Family Pet Guides

BUDGE R

Cyngor Sir Ddinbych
WEDITYNNU ALLAN O STOC .WITHDRAWN FROM STOCK
Denbighshire County Council

The author

David Alderton

David Alderton's lifelong interest in budgerigars started when he was given a stray pet bird as a boy. As well as breeding budgerigars, he has also studied their wild relatives in Australia, and has met fellow breeders in many parts of the world, including Europe, Japan, China and North America. He has chaired the National Council for Aviculture in the UK, and has broadcast both on radio and television about budgerigars. David has written widely about them in specialist publications, newspapers and magazines. His particular interest lies in the history of the different colour varieties. His books on pet care subjects have currently sold over four million copies worldwide, being available in more than 25 languages. He lives in Brighton, East Sussex.

ACKNOWLEDGEMENTS

The publishers would like to thank the following for their kind assistance in producing this book: Doug Austin, Keith Pask and Russell Wells.
Stuart Christophers at Ernest Charles & Co., bird seed suppliers.

BUDGERIGAR

DAVID ALDERTON

First published in 2002 by
Collins
an imprint of
HarperCollins*Publishers*
77–85 Fulham Palace Road
Hammersmith
London W6 8JB

The Collins website address is
www.collins.co.uk

Collins is a registered trademark of
HarperCollins Publishers Limited.

07 06 05 04 03 02
9 8 7 6 5 4 3 2 1

© HarperCollins*Publishers* Ltd 2002

David Alderton asserts the moral right to
be identified as the author of this work.

All rights reserved. No part of this
publication may be reproduced, stored
in a retrieval system, or transmitted, in
any form or by any means, electronic,
mechanical, photocopying, recording
or otherwise, without the prior
permission of the publishers.

A catalogue record of this book is
available from the British Library.

ISBN 0 00 712284 5

THIS BOOK WAS CREATED BY
SP Creative Design for
HarperCollins*Publishers* Ltd
EDITOR: Heather Thomas
DESIGN AND PRODUCTION: Rolando Ugolini

PHOTOGRAPHY:
Cover photographs by Dennis Avon.
All other photographs by Dennis Avon
with the following exceptions:
David Alderton: 2, 11, 13, 15, 65, 75,
83, 105, 121
Rolando Ugolini: 48, 52, 53, 55, 76,
79, 81, 89 (bottom), 93

COLOUR REPRODUCTION BY
Colourscan, Singapore
PRINTED AND BOUND BY
Printing Express Ltd, Hong Kong

Contents

LLYFRGELLOEDD SIR DDINBYCH DENBIGHSHIRE LIBRARIES	
C4600000322381	
L B C	02/10/2002
636.6864	£7.99
	RU

While every reasonable care was taken in the compilation of this publication
the Publisher and Author cannot accept liability for any loss, damage, injury
or death resulting from the keeping of budgerigars by user(s) of this
publication, or from the use of any materials, equipment, methods or
information recommended in this publication or from any errors or omission
that may be found in the text of this publication or that may occur at a future
date, except as expressly provided by law.

Introduction

In the space of little more than 150 years, the colourful budgerigar has become the most widely-kept pet bird in the world today, overtaking the canary as it has established a truly international following.

Budgerigars have proved themselves to be highly adaptable companions, easy to manage either in the home or a garden aviary. There is now a myriad of different colours and colour combinations, with today's domesticated budgerigars being far removed from their wild Australian ancestors. This is especially apparent in exhibition birds, which are larger and heavier than those kept as pets.

Other attributes of the budgerigar have also helped to assure its popularity. These birds have proved to be quite hardy, which is an important consideration when it comes to selecting aviary occupants in temperate parts of the world. Furthermore, they also live together well when kept in flocks, particularly if they are not breeding in these surroundings.

Few birds are easier to keep than budgerigars: their diet is comprised largely of seed, and they are not especially noisy or destructive, unlike many members of the parrot family. They can be tamed without great difficulty and can soon be persuaded to mimic sounds and talk. Easy to handle, alert and responsive, these popular parakeets appeal to people of all ages. A pet budgerigar is the ideal companion for someone living on their own, thanks to its lively chatter and friendliness, while keeping these birds in a garden aviary will appeal to the whole family.

Above: *A pet budgerigar can bring pleasure to all the family,*
however young.

CHAPTER ONE

Origins and varieties

Budgerigars are found across most of Australia, although they are absent from coastal areas, particularly on the eastern side of the continent as well as Tasmania. In the wild, they measure about 18 cm (7 in) and weigh just 29 g (1 oz), whereas their domesticated counterparts have evolved into slightly larger and definitely heavier birds, sometimes being twice this weight.

The name 'budgerigar' means 'good eating' in Aboriginal dialect, while the scientific name *Melopsittacus undulatus* translates as 'song parrot with the wavy markings' – a reference to the patterning extending down over the back and wings of these parakeets. As members of the parrot family, budgerigars appear to have no close relatives, even among other species occurring in Australia. Their closest relatives are probably the Grass Parakeets forming the genus *Neophema*, but they have never hybridized successfully together.

Little could the explorer and naturalist John Gould have anticipated the impact that these attractive parakeets would have when he returned to England from Australia with a pair in 1840. These were the first budgerigars to be seen alive in Europe although, prior to this, the species had been originally described

CHAPTER
ONE

in 1700. Even before Gould's introduction, however, their powers of mimicry had been discovered by a forger called Thomas Watling, who had been transported to the penal colony in Australia for his crime. Working alongside the doctor in his settlement, Watling taught the budgerigar to greet the physician, who was amazed when he discovered it was the bird that had uttered the words of greeting rather than Watling.

Gould's budgerigars passed into the care of his brother-in-law, Charles Coxen, and before long they were nesting. There was soon a growing demand among the rising middle classes in London and elsewhere, who wanted a budgerigar as a parlour pet, and ships carried these parakeets to Europe in substantial numbers. They proved to be hardy travellers, with mortality during the long sea journey remarkably low.

The emergence of colour mutations in the 1870s provided a huge boost to the interest in budgerigars, and speculation began, as such birds started to fetch amazing prices. Before long, commercial breeding establishments were being set up to cater for the massive demand for these parakeets, notably in France where as many as 100,000 birds were housed at some localities.

▌ The rise of showing

As colour varieties started to become more readily obtainable, so interest grew in the exhibition side of the hobby. The Budgerigar Club, founded during the 1920s, is the oldest establishment of its kind today, being responsible for overseeing the exhibition side of budgerigar-keeping in the UK. It gained a royal patron in the guise of King George V after changing its name to the Budgerigar Society which was deemed to be more socially acceptable in the 1930s.

Judging standards started to be established for these parakeets, describing not just their overall appearance or type, but also their pattern of markings and coloration. Since then, exhibition budgerigars have evolved noticeably, not just in the number of colour varieties that exist but also in terms of their appearance, being much larger in size today than in the past.

As new colours have emerged, so judging standards have been created to set out the features which are deemed to be desirable in these varieties. In order to do well at a show, however, it is essential that the birds themselves are always in top condition and not moulting.

Above: *This budgerigar is an exceptional example of its kind, having won the Best-in-Show award out of approximately 10,000 entries of birds of all types at a recent UK National Exhibition of Cage & Aviary Birds.*

CHAPTER
ONE

Famous owners

There have been a number of famous budgerigar owners over the past 150 years, including King George V, who founded an aviary of these popular parakeets which is still maintained at the royal residence of Sandringham in Norfolk. Others include the British war leader Sir Winston Churchill, who kept a budgerigar called Toby with him at 10 Downing Street, London. Toby was granted the exclusive privilege of being allowed to fly around the Cabinet Room. The composer Sir Malcolm Sargent had a novel way of holding the attention of his orchestras during rehearsals by conducting with his pet budgerigar perched on his baton.

Equally, the competitive side of budgerigar breeding has attracted its share of well-known supporters, especially from the world of sport. The late Formula 1 racing driver James Hunt as well as Geoff Capes, the British athlete who held the title of the strongest man in the world, have been amongst those who have exhibited their birds with significant success. Geoff himself has now progressed to being a highly-respected budgerigar judge as well.

A famous bird

Individual budgerigars have also become famous, none more so perhaps than Sparkie, a pet kept by a Mrs Williams in the north-east of England. She obtained Sparkie as a young bird and taught him over 550 words. These enabled him to repeat 358 different phrases and eight complete nursery rhymes, which he was encouraged to learn line-by-line.

Sparkie won a talking bird competition organised by the BBC in 1958, beating 2,768 other entrants. He was subsequently much in demand for personal appearances, and a recording that he made sold over 20,000 copies. He died in 1962 and can still be seen today in Newcastle's Hancock Museum.

BEHAVIOUR AND BIOLOGY

The highly social nature of budgerigars has led to them becoming very popular companions, while they will also agree well in groups, displaying strong flocking instincts. Their calls are quite musical and attractive, certainly when compared with the raucous screeching of many larger parrots, and this too is a factor which underlies their popularity as pets today.

Adaptability

Wild budgerigars inhabit some of the most inhospitable areas in the inhabited world, and in order to survive in such arid surroundings, they migrate widely through their extensive range. They seem to have an unerring ability to determine just when rainfall is imminent in an area, turning up just beforehand, and waiting for the seeds on the ground to grow and ripen, by which

Above: *Wild Australian budgerigars, as seen here, are much slimmer and smaller than today's domesticated strains.*

CHAPTER
ONE

stage pairs will be breeding in tree holes and other similar sites. Then, as the waterholes start to dry up and food becomes scarce, the budgerigars will move on again to another location, not returning to that area for months or sometimes years, depending on the conditions.

Even so, their numbers can fluctuate quite widely, being directly influenced by the availability of food and water. Faced with a widespread drought, many budgerigars are ultimately likely to die, but they can survive for as long as 130 days in the wild without drinking. It is this hardiness and adaptability that have helped them to settle and breed so well under a wide range of suitable domestic settings.

The significance of their coloration

Wild budgerigars are a natural light green in colour, and this affords these parakeets a distinct survival advantage. First, this coloration makes them hard to spot when perched in a tree. In flight,

Breeding behaviour

The freedom with which budgerigars will breed in the wild, increasing their numbers rapidly under favourable conditions, is also reflected in their readiness to breed either in cage or aviary surroundings. It is not uncommon for hen birds kept as pets to lay eggs on the floor of their cage. These should be left here until the hen loses interest in her clutch, rather than being taken away as this will simply encourage further egg-laying.

Similarly, in aviary surroundings, you need to be alert to the possibility that some pairs may want to nest, even in the absence of suitable nest boxes. They may attempt to gain access behind the lining in the aviary shelter, or even burrow beneath a loose paving slab, nesting in a subterranean fashion as a result, unless the chamber becomes flooded during heavy rain.

Above: *The wild budgerigar's green plumage and the contrasting wing patterning provide these parakeets with excellent camouflage when they are perching.*

budgerigars instinctively move in a very tight formation, which makes it harder for a bird of prey to pick off and target an individual from the flock, as they wheel and bank together. A bright yellow budgerigar among them would represent a relatively easy target, however, and so, not surprisingly, colour mutations are very rarely seen in the wild, in spite of being commonplace amongst domestic budgerigars. Studies in Florida, where flocks of wild budgerigars have become established from escapees, have revealed how predatory birds especially find it significantly easier to pick off budgerigars of colours other than green. As a consequence, flocks will revert back to the light green coloration of their ancestors because of this predation which imposes a direct selection pressure on them.

CHAPTER
ONE

VARIETIES OF BUDGERIGAR

Although odd examples of different colours have occasionally been recorded among wild flocks of budgerigars, exceeding few have contributed directly to the ancestry of any of today's domesticated colour varieties. The vast majority have all been evolved from mutations which arose in captive stock.

Those who saw the first domesticated colour variety, which was a Light Yellow bred during 1872 in Belgium, could not possibly have realised the significance of this event. Today, there are now many thousands if not actually millions of possible colour forms of the Budgerigar which can be bred, particularly when crested colour combinations are considered as well.

How the colours occur

In the case of green series birds, there are two colour pigment present in their feathers. An area of yellow pigment occurs in the outer layer of the plumage, with an inner core being comprised of black melanin pigment. Separating these two areas is the so-called blue layer, which reflects back light causing it to appear blue. When overlaid with the

Right: *A Light Green cock bird. This is a common colour in many domesticated budgerigars.*

yellow colour pigment, green coloration is seen, just as when blue and yellow paints are mixed together, but take away the yellow and the budgerigar appears blue.

On the other hand, should the black pigment be absent, then the bird will be yellow, whereas the Albino occurs when all colour pigment is missing, although the reflective blue layer remains intact. Without black behind it, however, it does not produce its distinctive coloration, but if you look very closely at an Albino in some lights, you will see a faint bluish hue to the plumage, because of the feather structure. The equivalent colours in green and blue series budgerigars are as set out in the table above.

Colour equivalents

Green series	Blue series
Light Green	Sky Blue
Yellows	Whites
Lutino	Albino
Grey Green	Grey
Green Violet	Visual Violet

Above: *Budgerigars with broken areas of colour are pieds. This pair consists of a Dark Green hen and a Violet Recessive Pied cock.*

CHAPTER
ONE

Blues

In 1878, the Sky Blue variety was first recorded, again in Belgium, but, apparently, it remained quite localized up until the early part of the twentieth century. Such birds caused a sensation when they were first shown in London during 1910 and, within a decade, they were being sent on the long journey back to budgerigar fanciers in Australia. The advent of this colour was ultimately to lead to a significant expansion in the potential range of colours that could be developed as, in due course, it could be combined with dark factor, pied and yellow-faced mutations, amongst others, creating new varieties.

Sky Blue

A pure white face, offset against the black throat spots and violet cheek patches are features of this mutation, with the colour of the body being a pure shade of sky blue. The markings on the head, back and wings are black, offset against white, while the tail feathers are a darker shade of blue.

Above: *A Cobalt Blue. This is the result of the dark factor being combined with blue coloration.*

Right: *The Sky Blue is still one of the most popular colour varieties of the budgerigar.*

The dark factor

Although this mutation is not actually a distinct colour as such, its presence has a very significant effect on a budgerigar's appearance, affecting its depth of coloration. This mutation has been observed in wild flocks of budgerigars, although its domestic development started in France during 1915. When this mutation occurs, there may be either one or two dark factors present, depending as to whether one or both chromosomes are affected (see pages 108–109). When there are two, the depth of coloration is darkened accordingly, as shown in the table below.

Right: *The Dark Green is intermediate in colour between the Light Green and Olive shades.*

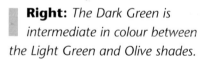

Dark factor equivalents

	Green series	Blue series
No dark factor	Light Green	Sky Blue
One dark factor	Dark Green	Cobalt
Two dark factors	Olive	Mauve

CHAPTER
ONE

The incredible 1930s

This was the decade more than any other which shaped the range of varieties that are available today, with Pied, Opaline and Grey forms being just some of the new mutations cropping up for the first time. It was also a period when even extinct mutations came back to life. One of the early colours which had been recorded was the Lutino, but unfortunately, this mutation had subsequently died out. Lutinos reappeared unexpectedly in the 1930s, both in English and Australian aviaries. On this occasion, however, different strains that were distinguishable on a genetic basis occurred.

Violets

One of the most sought-after and beautiful of all budgerigar colour varieties, the Violet is not the result of a single mutation. Instead, it represents a combination of the violet factor with mauve. It is also possible to have a green series equivalent, where olive is combined with the violet factor, and although such birds appear green in colour, they can play a valuable part in the breeding of visual Violets, whose plumage is of a deep violet shade.

Yellow-faced

It used to be thought that it was impossible for blue series budgerigars to display any yellow coloration, since it was the absence of this colour pigment that separated them from green individuals. This belief

Left: *A Violet cock bird. Pied and Yellow-faced Violets have also been bred.*

was shattered with the emergence of several different Yellow-faced mutations during the 1930s, however, with those of the deepest shade being described as Golden-faced. This characteristic could be combined with blue coloration of any shade. This meant that not only could Yellow-faced Sky Blues be bred, but also other combinations including Yellow-faced Cobalts.

Left: *This budgerigar combines the Yellow-faced characteristic with Grey coloration and Cinnamon markings.*

Right: *A Golden-faced Mauve, being of a richer shade than a Yellow-faced.*

Yellow and white forms

One of the most obvious distinguishing features that sets yellow budgerigars apart from their Lutino counterparts is their eye coloration, which is black rather than red. This distinction is especially significant in the case of the Dark-eyed Clear Yellow, which is otherwise very similar to the Lutino in appearance. The blue cere coloration of cock birds and the presence of a mask enables Yellows to be separated from both Dark-eyed Clears and Lutinos, which are unusual in having mauve ceres.

Similar distinctions also exist in the case of budgerigars having white plumage, with the legs and feet of the White itself being dark, compared with the pink coloration seen in both the Albino

CHAPTER
ONE

Above: *An Albino (left) and a Lutino. Both have red eyes and the lack of black pigment means they also have no throat spots.*

and the Dark-eyed Clear White. Although the Light Yellow was the first budgerigar mutation to be recorded, such birds have become scarce, with the Lutino now being far more widely-kept, just as in the case of Whites and Albinos. Dark-eyed Clears are also quite rare today.

Grey

Grey budgerigars first made their appearance during the 1930s, with today's Dominant Greys being descended from a single budgerigar bought in Melbourne, Australia. There was also a genetically-distinct recessive form of the Grey, which has since appeared to have died out, although it could always re-emerge in the future. Grey budgerigars are distinguished not just by their grey body coloration, but also by their grey cheek patches and black tail feathers. It has since been possible to combine this colour with other mutations as well, to create Grey Greens and Pied varieties, for example, as well as Cinnamon and Opaline forms.

Top right: *A normal Grey budgerigar. Its head markings are well-defined.*
Right: *An Opaline Grey. Note the difference in this wavy patterning.*

CHAPTER
ONE

▌Changes in patterning

It has not just been alterations in the Budgerigar's basic coloration that have occurred. There have also been significant changes in the depth and coloration of its markings.

Greywings
The emergence of the Greywing back in 1875, in Belgium, represented the first modification of the budgerigar's markings, which may also impact on the depth of its body coloration. This particular mutation alters the black wing markings to an attractive shade of grey and can occur in both blue and green series budgerigars. This dilution of the black pigment melanin also means that the body coloration is paler than normal, in the case of Greywings.

Clearwings
Clearwings have significantly paler wing markings than usual. They were first recorded from the aviaries of an Australian breeder in Sydney during 1930, and have since been bred in both blue and green series variants. Ideally, the colour of the wings should be as pale as possible, with little trace of the dark patterning associated with wild budgerigars.

Whitewings
The Whitewing mutation is linked with blue series coloration. Among the first variants of this type to be recorded were Whitewing Cobalts, which soon became very fashionable.

▌**Above:** *A Whitewing Cobalt hen. It is the colour of the wing and throat markings that is affected.*

Above: *A White Sky Blue (left), which can be distinguished from the Whitewing Sky Blue (right) by its paler body colour.*

CHAPTER
ONE

They were originally described as Royal Austral Blues as one of the first pairs to be bred was presented to King George V. Whitewing Violets, with their deep body coloration and pale wings are also a sought-after variety within this grouping.

Yellow-wings

The Clearwing equivalents in green series budgerigars are the Yellow-wings. Again, the basic body coloration is unaffected by this mutation, and it is possible to breed Yellow-wing forms of all shades of green, ranging from light green through dark green to olive, as well as a grey green variety which can be instantly recognised by the colour of its cheek patches. These are grey rather than violet, with the tail feathers also being grey, but there can be variance between individuals in their depth of coloration, depending as to whether the appearance has been influenced by any dark factor involvement.

Above: *The Yellow-wing characteristic is a feature of green series budgerigars.*

Clearflight

In this case, there is no noticeable change to the Budgerigar's overall coloration, other than that of the flight and tail feathers. These show no trace of dark pigment, and so are described as being clear. They may be either yellow or white, depending on the particular variety. In a few cases, such as the Lutino, the clearflighted mutation will not show up, because the coloration of these areas of plumage will inevitably be yellow, or white in the case of the Albino.

Cinnamons

The Cinnamon mutation modifies the melanin granules, so the black areas of the plumage become brown. This change extends not just to the patterning over the back and wings but also affects the spots around the face. Cinnamon coloration can be associated with both green and blue series budgerigars and also has the effect of lightening the body colour somewhat.

Opaline

The Opaline is a mutation which is not linked with coloration, although it tends to look most impressive in the case of varieties which have black body markings, emphasising the contrast

Above: *An Opaline Cinnamon hen.*

with so-called Normals. The first report of the Opaline originated from an immature wild hen budgerigar which was offered for sale in Adelaide in 1933. Other Opaline strains appear to have arisen independently in Europe.

The markings in the case of Opalines are less defined than in the case of Normals, especially on the sides of the head, with a clear V-shaped area between the wings. Unfortunately, a common problem that is seen in this variety today is the way in which unwanted patches of dark pigment may appear on the budgerigar's forehead. This fault is described as flecking.

Left: *An Opaline Yellow-faced Cobalt. The Opaline characteristic affects the bird's patterning.*

CHAPTER
ONE

Above: *The difference in markings between Normal and Opaline budgerigars can be clearly seen by comparing these two Grey Green cock birds, with the Opaline on the right.*

Fallows

Two distinctive forms of the Fallow mutation exist, being named after their respective countries of origin. The English Fallow can be easily distinguished from its German counterpart by the fact that it lacks the characteristic white ring of the iris, which is a feature of most adult budgerigars. The overall effect in both cases is similar, however, with the coloration being significantly lighter than usual, while the eyes may appear either reddish or plum in colour.

Lacewings

These budgerigars display cinnamon markings offset against either yellow or white coloration. They have red eyes and a mask, with the cheek patches themselves being pale violet. The tail feathers are also cinnamon brown in colour. The depth of colour between individuals may vary, depending on whether they have a dark factor ancestry.

Left: *A top Lacewing Yellow hen. The pale cere indicates she is not in breeding condition.*
Right: *This Clear Lacewing does not have obvious wing markings.*

CHAPTER
ONE

Spangles

The most significant change in the budgerigar's patterning of recent years has been the emergence of the Spangle mutation, again in Australia. It is now believed to have emerged originally in an aviary of budgerigars located in the state of Victoria during 1972, before being introduced to Switzerland in the 1980s, and thence to the rest of Europe and North America. The Spangle has proved to be dominant in its mode of inheritance (see page 111), and so it has proved possible to increase the numbers of these budgerigars rapidly to the extent that they are now commonly kept worldwide.

Single factor individuals always display darker patterning than their double factor counterparts. The basic markings are reversed in this case, with this change being most apparent over the wings. As a result, in green series individuals, the yellow areas are edged with black, with white replacing the yellow in blue coloured Spangles. This change applies to the tail feathers, too, which are often edged in black. The cheek spots have pale centres of the appropriate colour, being either yellow or white.

Left: *A Doub* *Factor Grey Spangle cock.*

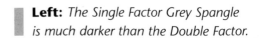

Left: *The Single Factor Grey Spangle is much darker than the Double Factor.*

Pieds

Two distinct types of pied budgerigar exist, both of which were originally recorded during the 1930s. The Australian Dominant Pied arose in 1935, again in Sydney. These budgerigars typically display either green and yellow or blue and white coloration across their bodies, with their patterning being highly individual, although it is relatively standardized in exhibition stock. Grey and yellow-faced characteristics are also not uncommonly seen in pieds.

The other type of pied is the smaller Danish Recessive, which was first reported in 1932 in Scandinavia. These pieds are easily identified by their dark, plum-coloured eyes which lack any iris around the pupil at their centres, as well as on genetic grounds (see page 109). They are bred in a similar range of colours. Those that are mainly light in colour are described as being lightly variegated, compared with those that have more prominent markings and are known as heavily variegated.

Left: *An Opaline Grey Green Dominant Pied cock.*

Left: *A Yellow-faced Grey Recessive Pied hen.*

Above: *A Sky Blue Dominant Pied cock, with pied areas being white.*

CHAPTER
ONE

Crested forms

Perhaps surprisingly, although they have a long history dating back to the 1930s and can be bred in association with any colour or pattern, crested budgerigars are still relatively uncommon. There are actually three different variants, of which the full circular crested is the most striking. The raised crest of feathers looks rather like a crown on the head. There is also a half circular form, where the crest should extend just over the front half of the head, plus a tufted variety, where the feathers are elongated to form a vertical crest, although, unlike the situation with cockatoos, these cannot be lowered at will.

Above: *This Opaline Grey Green cock has an even and well-balanced full circular crest.*

Left: *The evenness of the length of the feathers is an important feature of the crest, as shown by this Grey individual.*

New mutations and revivals

A quite recent development in the world of budgerigars has been the breeding of the Texas Clearbody, which is the first mutation of US origins. As their name suggests, these birds have pale body plumage, compared with their markings. Yet for many budgerigar breeders, the most significant new colour to emerge for many years is the Anthracite, a mutation first recorded in 1998 from Cologne, Germany. Its body coloration borders on black, along with the cheek patches and spots forming the mask. In fact, under natural lighting conditions, the Anthracite does appear to be black, and is certainly not just a darker grey variant.

Further study has now revealed the Anthracite to be an autosomal recessive character, in terms of its mode of inheritance. At present, its numbers are small, but it hoped that this new mutation will soon become firmly established on the list of budgerigar colours, and that other variants such as Anthracite pieds will also be created before long.

Breeders are also working to maintain some of the rarer colours which have evolved and yet are now considered to be in danger of dying out. These include the Slate, a mutation which is of British origins and first emerged in 1935. This characteristic can be combined with both green and blue series birds, with Slate individuals being of a more bluish tone than Greys and having dull blue rather than black tail feathers.

Right: *A Slate Cobalt hen. The Slate is one of the rarer budgerigar mutations, which actually modifies the coloration.*

CHAPTER TWO

Acquiring your bird

It is important to have a clear idea of what you are seeking before setting out to acquire a budgerigar. Otherwise, you could easily end up being disappointed with your choice. Are you looking for a pet bird or aviary breeding stock? Alternatively, you may be interested in exhibiting. All these factors will have a direct influence on where it will be best to seek out your new budgerigar.

Pet stores often have a number of young birds which are suitable as pets on offer, as may local breeders, but if you are interested in obtaining exhibition stock to start your own stud, then you will need to track down a breeder who specializes in such birds. This can usually be done through a national budgerigar organisation, which can often be located via the Internet, or through a reference library. Alternatively, exhibition breeders may be found through specialist bird-keeping magazines available on news-stands.

Tame adult budgerigars are sometimes offered for sale, rather than young birds. Such individuals will usually adjust well to a new home, but they are unlikely to expand their vocabulary significantly. Never be tempted to try to tame an older bird from an aviary however, because they rarely settle satisfactorily indoors.

▌ Recognising a young budgerigar

One of the most important considerations when purchasing a
budgerigar, either as a pet or for breeding purposes, is its age.
In the case of a pet bird, it is best to start out with a young
individual which will be about six weeks of age, and preferably
not older than nine weeks. There are several key indicators that
will enable you to be sure that you are obtaining a genuine
youngster. These are as follows:

■ Most colour varieties have wavy lines on the head, extending
right down to the cere, which is the fleshy area encompassing

▌ **Above:** *A budgerigar of eight weeks old can be seen on the
left, with an adult on the right. Note the characteristic bars
that are present above the young bird's cere.*

Right: *The barring is being lost and the cere is turning brown in this young Slate Sky Blue hen. The spots will become more prominent.*

the nostrils above the bill. This is why young budgerigars are described as barheads, up to the age of three months old, when they moult for the first time and this pattern is replaced by clear plumage. Their facial spots will also start to become more prominent at this first moult.

■ Even in the case of the few colours, such as the Albino, where this wavy patterning is absent, fledglings can generally be distinguished by the absence of a white ring around the outside of the eye. This only starts to develop when a young budgerigar is around 12 weeks of age.

■ Darker-coloured individuals usually display a dark brownish area on their upper bill when they first leave the nest. This disappears by the time they are about seven weeks old.

■ The cere coloration in the case of both sexes is purplish at this stage. However, young cock birds can usually be identified with relative ease because their ceres are more prominent and are a darker shade of purple, especially around the nostrils themselves, compared with young hens.

CHAPTER
TWO

Sex, temperament and age

Although budgerigars of either sex can talk, most pet-seekers prefer having a young cock bird, because they are reputed to be the best mimics and will certainly sing more than hens. Cock budgerigars also prove to be less destructive than hens when they come into breeding condition, and there is no risk of them suffering from laying unwanted eggs. They may start regurgitating seed to feed to their toys at this stage, however, which may become a problem.

There is virtually no difference between the different colours and varieties in terms of their temperament, although sometimes Recessive Pieds prove to be instinctively more flighty by nature than other varieties, and so are slightly harder to tame.

Ideal age

The ideal age to obtain a young budgerigar is as soon as it leaves the nest and is eating on its own, which is why it may be better to track down a breeder. This can usually be done quite easily through the advertisement columns of local newspapers. Arrange to see the chicks on offer first, and then you can pick one even while it is still in the nest, arranging to collect it at a later date. You are likely to find the largest choice available during the summer months, although budgerigars will breed throughout the year. Therefore it is possible to find chicks for sale during the winter but it may be harder to find a young bird of a particular colour.

Obtaining aviary stock

If you are seeking breeding stock for an outdoor aviary, then the late summer is probably the best time to acquire budgerigars. This is when breeders are most likely to be reducing their stock after the breeding season, and you will have a choice between early-reared youngsters and older birds.

While budgerigars can breed from the age of four to six months onwards, it is not recommended to encourage them to go to nest until they are virtually a year old, by which time they will be fully mature. They will carry on breeding for most of their lives, but the reproductive success of older birds, especially hens, will be lower, and the risk of complications, such as egg-binding (see page 00), increases. Therefore, ideally, you should try to avoid purchasing budgerigars aged over four years old for breeding purposes. An exception may be made in the case of a prize-winning older cock bird, since exhibitors are often unwilling to part with their best young birds, and yet an older bird may still be able to sire top-quality chicks when it is mated with a good-quality hen.

Although a breeder is likely to know the age of the birds being offered for sale, this will not apply in the case of a bird farm, and after an unrung budgerigar has moulted out into adult plumage, it will be impossible to tell its age reliably. You can generally tell the age of exhibition stock with certainty, however, because such birds are banded with closed rings which have the year of hatching encoded on them. A closed ring can only be fitted while the budgerigar is still in the nest (see page 103) and thereby provides a clear indication of the year of hatching. The breeder's initials and a sequential number, serving to identify the individual bird, are also likely to be evident on the ring.

Visit some shows

Before purchasing exhibition stock, it can pay dividends to visit a number of shows, so that you can familiarize yourself with the type of birds that are winning. It is also helpful to focus on a particular colour category, since most exhibition breeders specialize in specific varieties. This is because the features that make up a good strain of blues, for example, can be developed to best effect in this way.

CHAPTER
TWO

▌Buying on a budget

Good-quality exhibition budgerigars are likely to be considerably
more expensive than pet-type birds. This a reflection of the care
and time that have been devoted to developing their pedigrees.
It can help if you acquire most of your stock from just one or two
successful breeders at the outset, because buying exhibition
budgerigars from a number of different sources is likely to affect
the appearance of the chicks, whereas you should be able to
maintain a potentially prize-winning look if you stay with an
established strain.

Decide on your budget at the outset, rather than the number of
birds that you want. It is generally better to start out with relatively
few budgerigars of a higher quality than a greater number which
are average, simply because the likelihood of breeding top-quality

▌**Above:** *It is not only the appearance of exhibition birds that is
significant. Their bloodline can be just as important.*

Right: *The only way of confirming a budgerigar's age with certainty is from a closed ring. This one hatched in 2000.*

offspring in due course will be enhanced, as you will be working with better bloodlines.

While there are no certain routes to success on the show bench, being able to appreciate just what makes a top-quality exhibition budgerigar is vital. Without this image in your mind, even if you could persuade a top exhibitor to part with their best bird, the likelihood is that you would not be picking up top awards for long. The best budgerigar studs are those that have strength in depth, rather than just one or two outstanding individuals.

Managing an exhibition stud effectively calls for patience, and this is why generally, show classes are tiered, starting with those for beginners and passing through novices and intermediates up to champions. This allows the quality of your stud to progress over the years, and enables you to exhibit your budgerigars in classes against other owners with a similar level of experience.

Recognising healthy birds

Whether you are seeking a budgerigar as a pet or for an aviary, you need to ensure that the bird is fit and well. You can gain an insight into its condition by watching its behaviour.

■ Healthy budgerigars are lively and alert.

■ Their plumage usually appears sleek, although it may look more fluffy in young birds.

■ They should fly readily and never flutter to the floor, which may be the result of missing flight feathers, caused by the viral disease often described as French Moult.

CHAPTER
TWO

Handling a budgerigar

Assuming that the budgerigar that appeals to you seems to be generally fit, you should then carry out a closer examination with the bird in your hand, or in that of the vendor. People are often worried about holding budgerigars but it is not difficult to do, especially once you have practised a few times. It does pay to remember, however, that these parakeets have quite sharp bills which can inflict a painful nip and draw blood.

1 The bird's head always needs to be safely restrained. This can be done easily by holding the budgerigar so that its wings lie in the palm of your hand, with its head gently held between the first and second fingers.

2 The thumb and other fingers can be used to wrap around the bird's body although, generally, with the wings closed in the palm of the hand, a budgerigar will not struggle. Do not, however, press tightly with your fingers on the sides of the bird's neck, because you could inadvertently prevent it from breathing as a result.

Left: *Handling a budgerigar safely. When restrained in this way, the bird will not be able to bite or struggle, and you will be able to inspect most of its body easily, even holding out the wing, for example, to check for any signs of French Moult.*

Carrying out a general health check

When checking on a budgerigar's state of health, try to follow
the same procedure, starting at the head, so that, hopefully, you
will not overlook anything.

■ **Nostrils**
Should be evenly sized.

■ **Eyes**
Should be red or black
and bright, not glazed
over and dull.

■ **Cere**
Should be well coloured,
depending on age, sex
and variety

■ **Bill**
The upper bill should
fit snugly over the
lower part.

■ **Chest**
Breastbone should
be a bony ridge
with no hollows
on either side.

■ **Wings**
There should
be no loss of
flight feathers.

■ **Claws**
Should be well
formed on each toe
with none missing.

■ **Tail**
Needs to be full length
and not stunted, which can
be a sign of French Moult.

CHAPTER
TWO

The bill

Deformities do occur occasionally, and these may be an inherited problem. The upper bill should fit snugly over the lower part, but it can become overgrown or distorted, sometimes due to scaly face. This is caused by a mite boring into the tissue. In the early stages, it results in miniature snail-like tracks over the upper bill, often close to the cere, with distinctive coral-like growths soon emerging if it is left untreated. Undershot bills may result from poor nest hygiene, the upper bill curling round into the lower bill rather than overlapping it, so the lower bill grows out unchecked.

The eyes

These should be bright and either red or black, with no whitish glaze over the surface, which could indicate a cataract.

The cere

This should be well-coloured. Be cautious of an adult cock budgerigar that shows traces of brown on its cere near the nostrils, particularly if linked with evident weight loss.

The chest

You can determine a bird's condition by feeling its sternum, which runs down the centre of the body in the midline. This should be apparent as a bony ridge, with no distinctive hollows on either side, which indicate muscle wasting. Combined with a significant change in cere coloration, this can be an early indicator of an internal tumour. Breeders refer to weight loss here as 'going light', but this isn't a specific illness. In the case of a chick, it could be that the bird was weaned too young and has not been eating properly.

The wings

■ It is especially important with budgerigars to open out the wing, which can be done gently while the bird is still in your hand. These birds are especially prone to loss of flight feathers as youngsters, thanks to the illness known as French Moult. In older birds, these feathers may regrow in mild cases, but such birds represent a hazard to others if they are still infective. Look closely at the base of the feather shaft near where it enters the skin.

■ In the case of new feathers, this area appears pink when the feather is receiving a blood supply, and then becomes white. In the case of those budgerigars that have previously contracted French Moult, however, there will be small traces of dried blood evident in the feather shafts. It is not necessarily just the flight feathers that may be affected – sometimes the tail feathers, too, are lost.

■ Check the feathering around the vent, because if this area is stained, it indicates that the bird has probably suffered a recent digestive upset, which can be another cause of 'going light'.

The legs
Finally, look at the legs and feet. In the case of an unrung bird, if these appear quite heavily scaled, this is often a sign of old age, although if the legs seem encrusted, the budgerigar will be suffering from a mite infestation, which is usually linked with scaly face. Where there is a leg band, check the information here and that the ring can be moved easily, with no sign of swelling in this area. Occasionally, for no apparent reason, a budgerigar's leg will swell up around the ring, which will then need to be removed (see page 125).

It is also worth checking the ball of the foot for any sign of inflammation. When examining the feet, there must be a well-formed claw on each toe, especially in the case of exhibition birds. A single missing claw prevents a bird from being shown, although its absence causes no significant handicap to the budgerigar itself. A distorted claw, often the result of an injury, will also ruin an individual's exhibition potential; it may need to be cut back regularly to prevent it from becoming overgrown.

CHAPTER THREE

Housing and equipment

There are numerous different designs of cages now available for budgerigars, but not all of them are particularly suitable for these active parakeets. Overall, the most important consideration when deciding how best to house your pet will be to give it as much flying space as possible.

Do not choose one of the small circular cages on the market, but opt instead for a large rectangular design. If you have the space, you may even want to consider obtaining one of the stylish indoor flight cages which are mounted on castors, making them easy to move for cleaning purposes.

▌ Cage designs

Apart from size, the ease of cleanliness is a very important consideration. Some designs come in two sections, with the top mesh section being separated easily from the plastic base – what you do have to check, however, is that your pet cannot slip out and escape when you are cleaning its quarters with this type of set-up. It is often possible to clean the floor tray and then slide this up to form a false floor to the top section in order that the base can be detached and washed off if necessary, without any risk of the budgerigar escaping.

CHAPTER
THREE

Right: *Modern materials have helped to ensure that* cages can be easily cleaned, but beware of distorting plastic by washing it with very hot water.

Hygiene

Most cages now have bars that are covered with white epoxy resin, which means that not only do they not rust readily, but they are also easy to keep clean simply by wiping them over with a damp cloth or special cage wipes. The base unit, being made of moulded plastic, also adds to the overall high standard of hygiene, especially because there will be no gaps where mites could establish themselves.

Bars and perches

If possible, always choose a cage that has horizontal rather than vertical bars, as budgerigars like clambering around their quarters, and this is much harder if the bars are upright. The perches supplied in cages today are made of plastic, and most budgerigars appear to find such perches uncomfortable after a short period of time, to the extent that they will often remain clinging on to the

Spare parts for sectional cages

Since the two parts of the cage are held together by plastic clips, enquire about the availability of spares because, over a period of time, these may become brittle and snap. It may be worthwhile acquiring a spare set or two at the outset, since the cage should last throughout your budgerigar's life, which may be a decade or even longer.

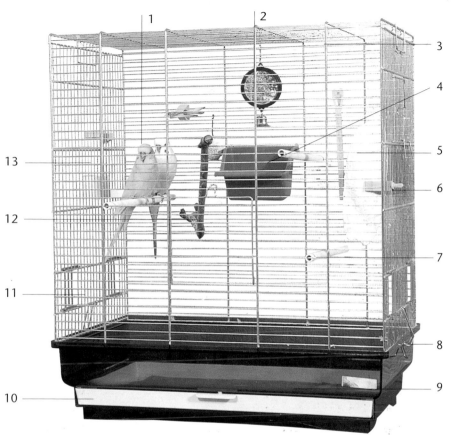

Above: *A suitable cage for indoor birds, this has plenty of room to exercise the wings, is easy to clean, well ventilated and well equipped.* **1** *A couple of birds to keep each other company* **2** *A mirror with a bell* **3** *Horizontal bars for safety* **4** *Clean raised bird feeder* **5** *Cuttlebone* **6** *Strong safety clips for attaching items to the cage* **7** *Several strong well-secured perches* **8** *Strong metal clips to keep the cage attached to the base* **9** *Raised plastic base to avoid overspill* **10** *Removable litter tray for convenience which can be pulled out at the front for cleaning* **11** *Cage doors that should be padlocked ideally* **12** *Natural wooden perch* **13** *Regularly cleaned water feeder.*

CHAPTER
THREE

Door fastenings

As a final check before buying a cage, examine the door fastening. This can be a surprising point of weakness in a number of designs, in spite of the fact that it is critical for the budgerigar's safety. As a further precaution, you may want to buy a small combination padlock so you can keep the door closed as required.

sides of the cage for long periods. Such perches must therefore be replaced, using safe, fresh branches which your budgerigar can gnaw (see page 64), helping to keep its bill in trim.

It helps if these perches are cut carefully so that they will fit into the plastic cups provided to hold the original perches in place. Not only does this look more attractive but it will also prevent the bars of the cage becoming distorted and bent. Perches cut from dowelling are no better than plastic, simply because they are of constant diameter. This can lead to inflammation of the inner ball of the feet, because the same part of the budgerigar's foot remains in contact with the perch. Some cages also come with a swing fitted. If your budgerigar appears to like resting here, then the swing can be left in the cage, but otherwise it should be removed rather than cluttering up the available space.

▌ Siting the cage

It is important to have an idea of where in your home you intend to keep your new pet. Never choose a location directly in front of a window, because even on just a warm day, the strength of the sun magnified by the window glass can easily prove to be a deadly combination. Similarly, do not keep your budgerigar in the kitchen, not only on grounds of hygiene, but also because birds are very susceptible to fumes given off by non-stick cookware if

Above: *Budgerigars need perches that they can grip easily, and therefore their diameter must not be too narrow.*

CHAPTER
THREE

Left: *Although sold for budgerigars, cylindrical cages of this type give the birds very little flying space. Rectangular designs are better.*

this overheats, and they will die within minutes as a result.

By choosing a location such as the living room where you spend much of your time, your budgerigar will soon become used to your presence. Try to position the cage so that it is approximately at eye level, which will make the taming process easier. It is not a good idea to place the cage in the centre of the room, however, because this can be disturbing for most birds. They prefer a location alongside a wall, where they will be out of a draught. Put a sheet of perspex or a similar barrier behind the cage in order to prevent soiling the wall covering. If you do not have a suitable piece of furniture on which to stand the cage, it is usually possible to purchase a stand, although this is not necessarily a good idea if you have young children, as they might accidentally pull the stand and cage over when trying to see the budgerigar.

Other equipment

You will need some other items of essential equipment for your budgerigar, including the following:

Feeders and drinkers
Many cages come equipped with these, although, like the perches, they are not always ideal. While tubular drinkers are

Left: *These plastic containers, complete with clips, are normally filled with water. If used for seed, beware as this can become stuck at the entrance to the spout, forming a blockage.*

good for water, even those with expanded bases are not entirely safe for dispensing seed. This is because the spout can easily become blocked, and although it may appear as though your pet has access to adequate food, the seed is actually out of reach. It is therefore safer to provide seed in an open container, which cannot become jammed in this fashion.

Young birds, however, may be reluctant to feed from a covered food pot, so watch carefully at first to ensure that your budgerigar is eating properly – otherwise, place the pot nearer the floor if it is adjacent to a perch, and sprinkle seed on the floor here. This should encourage the bird to recognise the container as a source of food and eat without difficulty.

Plastic surrounds

Covered food pots are favoured because they help to prevent seeds and husk being scattered outside the cage, and, as a further precaution

1

2

3

Right: *A variety of smaller feeders are available, which can be fixed near a perch or stood on the floor of the budgerigars' quarters. **1** Suspended feeder with wire supports **2** Cage seed hopper with self-closing lid **3** Plastic hook-on feeder **4** Ground feeder.*

4

to reduce the potential mess in the vicinity of the cage, you may want to fit a plastic surround around the base. However, try to do this in such a way that it is not in direct contact with the bars because it is otherwise possible for a budgerigar to become caught up in this surround by the tips of its claws.

Climbing ladders

Young budgerigars seem especially vulnerable to accidents because of their inquisitive natures and, consequently, it is not recommended to provide them with climbing ladders until they are six or nine months old. Otherwise, what can happen is that the budgerigar may manage to end up being caught between the rungs, as a result of its relatively small size.

Above: *Budgerigars will use plastic ladders readily, but these toys need to be hooked firmly in position, whether they are used inside or outside the cage.*

Hook-on pots for grit

It is a good idea to have a small hook-on pot for grit, which can be fitted in an easily accessible position over the bars of the budgerigar's cage.

Toys

When selecting toys of any type, always check that they are reasonably robust and also easy to clean. One of the most popular types of toy for budgerigars is a mirror which fits inside the cage; this may have a bell attached as well. You will need to check that cock birds, in particular, do not persistently feed their reflection when in breeding condition – otherwise remove the mirror for a few weeks until this phase passes. The same applies if the budgerigar displays to other toys in a similar fashion.

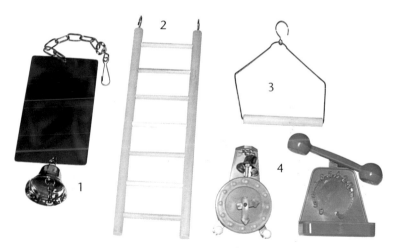

Above: *A few toys from the vast array available. Most useful are: **1** Bells and mirror with a chain **2** Ladder **3** Swing **4** Plastic mobile toys with moving parts for the bird to play with.*

CHAPTER
THREE

There are some toys, such as balls, that can simply be placed on the floor of the bird's quarters. These are likely to become soiled quite rapidly, however, and therefore it is important to ensure that they can be cleaned easily. One item that often turns out to be a very popular toy, in spite of not being sold for this purpose, is a simple ping-pong (table tennis) ball – it is lightweight and easy to clean.

Clips and cuttlebones

Another item that you will need is likely to be a clip to hold a cuttlebone (see page 81) in place. This helps to prevent the cage bars becoming distorted by pushing the cuttlebone through them. It also means that it is less likely to be soiled if it can be positioned in such a way that your budgerigar can reach the cuttlebone but is unable to perch on it.

Above: Mirrors are yet another popular toy for keeping most budgerigars busy and amused. Some designs are embellished with items such as sliding beads, as shown here.

An outdoor aviary

Many people who start with a pet budgerigar often find that their interest grows to the extent that they decide to set up an outdoor aviary. This is now quite straightforward, thanks to those companies that manufacture such housing in sectional form. You can generally choose from a variety of designs, or plan an aviary to your own dimensions, using a set of standardized panels for this purpose. It is well worth considering the designs offered by several aviary manufacturers before arriving at a decision. If possible, visit them so that you can see the standard of workmanship.

When comparing prices, be sure that you are making accurate comparisons, as some firms offer aviaries made of weather-

Above: *Budgerigars can generally live very well together in aviary surroundings, although such birds are not normally as tame as household pets.*

proofed timber, while others use untreated wood. The type of
wood used is also significant. Whereas ordinary treated softwood
timber may last 15 years without starting to show signs of rot,
tanalized timber, which is pressure treated so that the preservative
penetrates to a much greater extent, should remain free of rot for
over 50 years. Although it is more expensive initially, an aviary
made of tanalized timber will be a much better investment.

Aviaries consist of two parts: an outdoor component, comprised
of a wire mesh framework, known as the flight, and an indoor
shelter, which is where the budgerigars are fed and should be
encouraged to roost overnight. This can usually be achieved by
ensuring that the interior of the shelter is light and that the perches
here are fixed at a generally higher level than in the flight, as birds
will seek out the highest vantage points for roosting purposes.

Aviary construction

You should always check on possible planning restrictions before
starting to build an aviary although, in most cases, it will not be
necessary to seek official permission. When deciding where to
site the aviary, bear the following points in mind:

■ It is enjoyable to be able to watch the budgerigars in their
flight from inside your home.

■ The aviary should be constructed in a sheltered locality,
preferably out of the direction of the prevailing wind.

■ It should not be located at the front of your home, where it is
likely to attract vandals.

■ Try to allow for expansion, as you may want to increase the
size of the aviary at some stage.

■ If you are thinking of keeping exhibition budgerigars in the
future, it helps to have a location where it will be relatively easy
to have a power supply run out to the structure.

■ It will be very much harder to build the aviary on a slope;
choose level ground if possible.

Above: *A typical outdoor aviary for budgerigars. The presence of the safety porch should eliminate the risk of any birds escaping from the aviary, while the blockwork sunk beneath the ground helps to exclude unwelcome rodents.*

CHAPTER
THREE

▌ Building the aviary

1 Start by marking out the site carefully, using sand or posts and string, so that you can see the area that will need to be prepared.
2 Then, with a sharp spade, cut away any turf, which can be put on one side in a shady spot.
3 You will need to prepare the footings for the aviary by digging a trench around the perimeter to take the supporting blocks, down to a depth of at least 30 cm (12 in). Above ground, you may want to use bricks that give a more attractive appearance to create a low wall on which the frames can rest.
4 These footings will need to dry thoroughly before the aviary can be erected. Try to avoid carrying out this stage in the construction process when the weather is likely to be wet or the temperature drops below freezing, as this will obviously affect the bonding of the mortar, although covering the area with sacks may help to give some protection if necessary.
5 It is usually easier to work on the floor covering for the base, rather than starting to erect the aviary at this stage. The shelter area is normally made of concrete, which should be laid on a well-compacted bed of hardcore, with a damp-proof membrane of heavy-duty polythene set into it.
6 It is also a good idea to lay a layer of aviary mesh in the base, before placing the hardcore on top, so as to deter any rodents, such as rats, from attempting to dig their way into the structure.
7 The base of the flight can be made in a similar way, but drainage here will be very important to prevent the floor from being flooded when it rains. As a result, the concrete will need to be sloped towards a small drainage hole at the far end of the flight. You may need to employ a plasterer for this purpose – to ensure that the water drains away rapidly without pooling on the floor. The advantage of concrete is that it is easy to clean and disinfect, whereas other floor coverings, such as gravel, can

Right: *It is possible to convert a garden shed, or, alternatively, you can invest in a purpose-built birdroom, so that there is space to set up special breeding cages. Artificial heating and lighting may need to be incorporated into these surroundings.*

easily harbour disease. However, as a less permanent option than concrete, paving slabs can be used to create the floor covering. They can be kept clean without great difficulty but must be bedded down carefully and the gaps between the slabs filled with mortar.

Assembling the structure

It helps to have someone else to assist in erecting the aviary sections, although some manufacturers will undertake to build the structure on site for you if required. The simplest way of anchoring the panels together and to the base is to use frame fixers, driven through the timber, although using bolts for the frames is better, simply because it will make it easier to dismantle the sections in the future if you move to a new home. Do not forget to fix washers before the nuts, and keep them well-oiled to prevent them from rusting prematurely.

The way in which the frame is assembled is very important; you must keep the timber out of reach of the budgerigars' bills. Always put the panels together so that the mesh, rather than the framework itself, is on the inner face of the flight. Once the flight is assembled, the shelter can be erected with the front being put in place first, attaching to the flight, with the sides, back and roof following.

Aviary access

There is no need to worry about hanging the doors at this stage. It will be easier to do so later, once the perches have been fitted into the aviary, but it is important to have worked out how you will enter the aviary. There is a real risk that if you have a door connecting the aviary direct with the outside world, then a budgerigar could easily escape at some point when you enter. This can be prevented by incorporating a safety porch into the aviary design.

A safety porch usually takes the form of a mesh-covered area, measuring 90 cm (3 ft) square, which fits around the door leading into the aviary shelter. The arrangement of the doors is significant, to give you easy access into the interior. The door of the safety porch should be fitted so that it opens outwards rather than into the porch. There needs to be a bolt on its inner side, so that you can close this door securely before opening the door leading directly into the aviary shelter, which is hinged to open inwards. Any budgerigars that do slip past you will then be confined in the safety porch, from where they can be returned without difficulty into the aviary itself. Once in the shelter, you can then gain easy access to the flight through a connecting door, which again opens outwards.

The other entry point of concern will be the way in which the budgerigars themselves move back and forth between the flight and the shelter. It is usually recommended to cut a wooden platform into the front of the shelter at a reasonably high point for this purpose. It helps to fit this quite close to one of the sides of the aviary, so that you can then incorporate a piece of plywood set on runners and attached to a thick strand of wire

Landscaping

Although it is not possible to grow plants within the aviary because they will be destroyed by the budgerigars, and attempts at incorporating a grass floor in the flight are unlikely to be successful as it is soon likely to turn to moss, careful planting around the aviary will enhance its appearance. Climbing plants can be grown on trelliswork on the shelter, softening its images, while attractive borders can be devised around the base of the structure.

Be sure to keep most plants out of reach of the budgerigars, however, since many that are commonly grown, including bulbs such as daffodils, are likely to be poisonous to the birds. Some annuals, notably nasturtiums (*Tropaeolum majus*), can be trained up the outer vertical supports of the flight, to provide localized colour. Beware of growing perennial climbers, however, because their weight may damage the structure over a period of time.

Above: *It will take at least a year or so for the surrounding landscape planting to develop fully, helping the aviary to blend into the garden landscape.*

CHAPTER
THREE

extending out through the side of the aviary mesh. This will enable you to keep the birds confined as required in one part of the aviary, which can be useful if you are trying to catch particular individuals or bring in new perches.

Natural lighting is important in the shelter, because the budgerigars will otherwise be reluctant to enter, but panels of glass should be covered with mesh surrounds, held in place with battening so that there will be no risk of the sharp edges of mesh causing the budgerigars any harm. Similarly, in the flight itself, the mesh should be covered with hardwood battening around its edges.

Perching

The perches need to be positioned to give the birds plenty of flying space, and therefore, for this reason, they must be fixed across the flight. However, they must not be too close to the mesh at the far end of the flight or they may cause the budgerigars' tail feathers to rub against the mesh and become damaged. Natural branches are recommended for perches, with the budgerigars usually nibbling off the bark. Therefore it is important that these are cut only from trees that will not be poisonous and have not been sprayed recently with chemicals.

Fruit trees, such as apple, are a good choice, whereas trees whose branches grow relatively straight, such as sycamore, can also be useful. Some variance in the diameter of the perches is important but, on average, the majority of the branches used should be wide enough to allow the budgerigar's toes to curl around them without the hind toes coming into direct contact with the front ones. It is always a good idea to wash the branches off thoroughly, having cut them to size, just in case they have been soiled by wild birds whose droppings could represent a threat to the budgerigars' health.

Do not be tempted to force the perches into place through the aviary mesh because, over a time, this will weaken it and can

Above: *Easy access, both in and out of the shelter, is very important in order to persuade the budgerigars to roost in this part of the aviary at night.*

cause the strands to break. They should be attached instead to the vertical uprights in the aviary, by means of wire strands. These need to be held firmly in place, either by twisting them around the uprights or attaching them with netting staples, rather than attempting to nail them in place, since the nails will almost inevitably cause the branches to split. It is also a good idea to cut a crown of branches, which can be mounted vertically in a pot on the aviary floor, offering budgerigars other perching opportunities.

**CHAPTER
THREE**

A slightly different arrangement is often used in the shelter, with lengths of dowelling set in racks so they do not overhang each other. This enables more birds to perch within a more confined area, but natural branches can be used as well. It is easier to mount perches here in any event, as they can be fitted into wooden blocks with notches cut into them, stuck at the appropriate height on the sides of the shelter as supports.

Weather-proofing the aviary
Although budgerigars are hardy birds, they still need adequate protection from the worst of the weather. Therefore, once the aviary is completed, it is a good idea to add translucent plastic sheeting or some type of roof covering over the first 90 cm (3 ft) of the flight closest to the shelter. This must be sloped so that rainwater will run away via guttering fitted at the lowest edge, rather than pouring down into the flight itself. The water can be channelled away into a garden water butt or a soakaway.

Translucent plastic sheeting on the sides of the flight will also offer the birds protection against the wind. There are specialist fitments that should be used to hold the plastic in place, and it is worth acquiring an ultra-violet resistant grade as, otherwise, it will become fragile and will eventually break up

Left: *Large hoppers will be required for budgerigars being housed in groups in aviaries. There are various designs available, suitable for different types of foods.*

Painting the interior

If you want to lighten the interior of the aviary by painting it, then a light emulsion paint should prove safe. However, as an additional safeguard, do not paint the battening that the budgerigars are most likely to gnaw.

because of prolonged exposure to sunlight.

The roof of the shelter needs to be sealed as necessary and covered with two layers of heavy-duty roofing felt. Again, it will be a false economy to rely on a cheap grade, because this is likely to split quite quickly, allowing water to penetrate through the roof into the shelter. When fixing the roofing felt in place, use special nails for this purpose and tape down the joints to minimize the risk of the felt being ripped in high winds. Always overlap the top layer over the bottom, rather than the other way round, so there will be no risk of rainwater running back under the joint and reaching the timber beneath.

Insulating an aviary

Within the shelter itself, it can be a good idea to insulate the structure. This can be done very simply using insulation quilt, although take the recommended precautions when working with this material. You can then apply either oil-tempered hardboard, with the shiny side outwards, or thin plywood over the quilt, fixing this in place with panel pins. Hardboard tends to be less durable, however, so it may be a useful precaution to add hardwood battening around the edges, to deter the birds from nibbling at it. Although budgerigars are far less destructive than most members of the parrot family, they can inflict considerable damage over a period of time with their persistent gnawing. The battening will also provide a barrier to mice, which may otherwise seek to set up home in the lining of the aviary.

CHAPTER
THREE

▌ Constructing your own aviary

Although it is generally not cost effective to construct your own aviary from scratch, compared with buying the panels, it may be worthwhile if you have a particular design in mind. Even so, although most aviaries tend to be rectangular, there are some octangular styles now available commercially, which are suitable for sheltered localities, with an indoor area for the budgerigars at their core. If you do decide to go ahead and construct your own aviary, then the guidelines below will apply.

Construction guidelines

■ Choose timber that is at least 37.5 mm (1½ in) square, and preferably 50 mm (2 in) for larger flights.

■ The mesh can be 19 gauge (19 G), although thicker 16 gauge is likely to be more durable.

■ The individual strands should be no bigger than 2.5 x 1.25 cm (1 x ½ in) and preferably 1.25 cm (½ in) square to prevent mice from gaining access to the aviary.

Expansion into a birdroom

Many people starting out with budgerigars breed their birds in the aviary. However, if you are interested in exhibiting, you will need to choose pairs carefully and keep them apart from the other birds in breeding cages in order to ensure the parentage of their chicks. This is when a birdroom will prove to be very useful, allowing you to incorporate not just breeding cages but also, possibly, an indoor flight for young birds and storage facilities for seed and equipment.

While it is possible to convert an existing shed into a separate birdroom, the most convenient arrangement is to have a combined birdroom, which also incorporates the aviary shelter. Most birdrooms are therefore L-shaped, with the far end serving as the shelter area for the flight. This part is partitioned off by a mesh barrier incorporating a door, while the remaining area in the birdroom gives you free access to the breeding cages, seed and other items. Since you will enter the aviary itself via the birdroom, no separate safety porch is required in this instance.

An inner wire door to the birdroom is a useful precaution, however, just in case a budgerigar has slipped out into the birdroom area. In addition, it will also be possible for you to leave the outer door open for ventilation purposes when the weather is hot, without any risk of cats or other creatures gaining access to the birdroom.

Heating

In temperate areas, you may need to heat the birdroom if the birds are breeding during the colder months. The safest, most economical option is an electrical tubular heater of the type used in greenhouses, set under thermostatic control. Insulate the structure as far as possible, with draught excluders on the door helping to reduce heating costs. Fan heaters are not suitable as they will soon become choked by dust. This can be significantly reduced by means of an ionizer, which not only precipitates dust from the air but also kills harmful microbes in the atmosphere.

Lighting

This is required if you are breeding budgerigars in the winter because of the drastic reduction in day length. It will also allow you to attend to the birds' needs after dark without disturbing them unduly. The lights should be set under the control of an automatic dimmer switch, so that the level of illumination will fall off gradually rather than suddenly plunging the birdroom into darkness and leaving adult birds stranded away from their chicks.

CHAPTER FOUR

Looking after budgerigars

Part of the reason underlying the budgerigar's popularity today is the ease with which these parakeets can be cared for, either in the home or in aviary surroundings. Their feeding needs are quite straightforward, with special seed mixes for them being available not just in the usual pet outlets, but also from many mainstream supermarkets, where you can purchase a range of fresh foods that are suitable for budgerigars, including apples and carrots.

B udgerigars will always travel better within the confines of a box rather than a cage, in which they can flap about and may end up injuring themselves. A special wooden carrying box is therefore extremely useful for transporting your budgerigars. This is really an essential purchase if you have an aviary, as you will probably be moving the birds in and out of these surroundings, possibly on a frequent basis, both for breeding and for exhibition purposes.

In the case of a pet budgerigar, however, most pet stores will provide a special cardboard box with air holes for a short journey home. These boxes are not really suitable for a lengthy trip because some budgerigars attempt to gnaw and enlarge the air holes to escape from the carrier. Keep the box close to you to

CHAPTER
FOUR

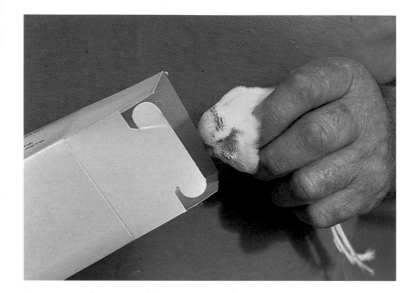

Above: *Special cardboard carrying boxes can be used for short journeys. Check the air holes and then seal the flaps.*

ensure that this does not happen. It is also important to check that the ends of the box are folded down properly and are stuck in place with some sticky tape as a further precaution.

Settling in

If possible, always make sure that everything is ready for your pet in advance. It is often recommended that you wash the cage and allow it to dry first in order to ensure that it is thoroughly clean. This advice applies especially in the case of a cage that has been on display in a shop alongside other birds, and also if it is secondhand. When buying a secondhand cage, try to find out about the fate of the former occupant. It certainly should be disinfected as a precautionary measure. There are special avian disinfectants now on the market, which can be recommended for this purpose.

In the case of budgerigars that are to be kept in an aviary rather than in your home, it is usually a good idea to house them in a suitable flight cage for about a fortnight before allowing them into the aviary.

During this period, you can treat the birds with a spray that is specifically intended to kill avian mites and lice. These can be spread easily in the confines of an aviary and may prove very difficult to eliminate, as in the case of red mite (see page 120). You can also check during this time that the budgerigars are eating well and appear to be healthy. Any warning signs of illness are most likely to become apparent during this period following the stress of a change in environment. With a young bird especially, which will not have been on its own before, you need to ensure that it can find its food easily.

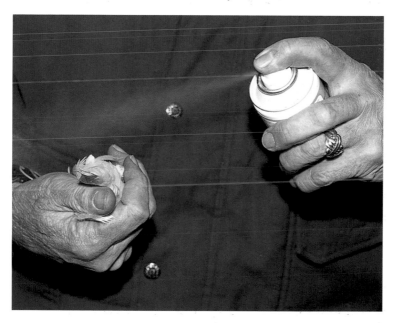

Above: *Use a special avian aerosol to kill mites and lice. Always read and follow the instructions carefully.*

CHAPTER
FOUR

Electrolytes and probiotics

You can help to settle in new arrivals by using electrolyte and probiotic products. Electrolytes help to maintain the balance within the body, in terms of key chemical constituents. Probiotics, on the other hand, consist of beneficial bacteria, which help to complement those already present in the digestive tract. A move coupled with new food can alter the balance within this part of the body, allowing harmful microbes to gain access to the body and cause illness.

Probiotics serve to reinforce the bird's own immune system when it is vulnerable. There are various types on the market, which can be administered easily in most cases through the bird's drinking water, sometimes being combined with electrolytes which can be given in a similar way. These products are also valuable for budgerigars recovering from illness, especially after a course of antibiotics, which is likely to depress the numbers of beneficial bacteria in the digestive tract. Many exhibitors also use them for birds that have recently returned from shows.

▮ Foodstuffs

In the wild, budgerigars feed on the seeds of grasses, and today's domesticated strains are given a similar diet, consisting of small cereal seeds. Most budgerigar mixes consist of the following two types of seed:

■ **Oval seeds** with pointed ends, which are plain canary seed
■ **Round seeds** in a mixture are likely to be millets of different types. These may include the relatively small, yellowish Japanese millet, and the larger, paler pearl white and red millets, recognisable by their coloration.

Other ingredients in some mixes include groats, which are the dehulled form of oats. This is quite a broad, long seed and relatively

Above: *A typical budgerigar seed mixture, comprised of millets, distinguishable by their rounded shape, and plain canary seed.*

fattening, so it should only be offered in relatively small quantities.

Although budgerigars thrive on a basic diet, they will benefit from other ingredients that are not present in a typical seed mixture. This is because these seeds are deficient in certain key ingredients, such as some essential amino acids which are key components of protein. Lysine, for example, is one of these compounds, along with methionine, and is necessary for good feathering.

Below: *There are a number of special seed mixtures now available, usually being marketed as tonic seed mixes.*

Right: *Millet sprays are very popular with budgerigars and can be offered either in their dried state or after being soaked (see page 78).*

CHAPTER
FOUR

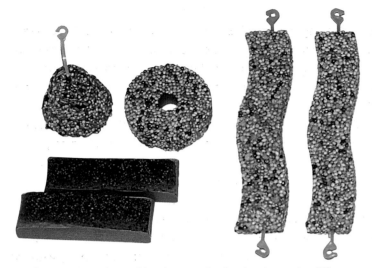

> **Above:** *A variety of food treats for budgerigars, in different shapes. The circular design fits around a perch, whereas others can be hung up in the birds' quarters.*

It is possible to supplement these items by means of other foodstuffs and, although they are not widely used, there are complete foods for budgerigars. These are available as small granules, which, although more expensive than seed, have no waste attached to them in the form of husk, and obviate the cost of using any other supplement. However, the problem can be to persuade the budgerigars to switch from seed to granules. Young birds, whose food preferences are less firmly established than those of older individuals, may be weaned more easily on to this type of food.

Providing food and water

Whether you are using seed or granules, the food must be kept dry and free from contamination by the birds' droppings. Open feeders, therefore, are not recommended, especially in aviary surroundings where the birds will often sit in the food bowl when feeding. It is much better to use a special hopper for seed. These are available in various sizes, depending on the number of birds in the aviary. In most designs, the husks collect in a tray beneath the seed reservoir rather than accumulating on the floor of the shelter.

Plastic hopper bases can be combined with clean jam jars to create hoppers. These are commonly used in breeding cages rather than aviary surroundings, overcoming the need to feed the birds every day. It is vital that the jam jar is not tilted forwards when inverted, because this can obstruct the flow of seed into the base, with potentially fatal consequences if the blockage is not spotted. The same applies in the case of tubular feeders, which can be attached to the outside of a cage, with the spout liable to becoming blocked in this instance.

Below: *Soft food should be provided in a container. All perishable foodstuffs need to be offered separately from dry seed in containers that can be washed easily.*

CHAPTER
FOUR

Soaked seed

Dry seeds do not figure regularly in the diet of budgerigars in the wild as they prefer ripening seeds. Fresh foods are therefore not surprisingly an important part of the diet of domesticated budgerigars. Nutritionally, such foods tend to be superior although in this state they will be perishable. This is why seed and, indeed, prepared foods must be stored in the dry to prevent them from turning mouldy.

Even soaked seed is highly beneficial to budgerigars and will usually be eaten in preference to dry seed. Soaking helps to soften the seed and stimulates the germination process, causing changes in the chemical composition. The protein and Vitamin B levels increase, with these changes making soaked seed especially valuable when there are young birds in the nest. It can also be beneficial for budgerigars recuperating from illness, as it is more easily digested than hard seed.

Soaking seed

Only prepare sufficient seed for a single feed in order to prevent any risk of it turning mouldy.

1 Simply rinse the required quantity under a running tap and then tip into a bowl before pouring on hot, but not boiling, water. Leave to stand overnight.

2 The seed should then be sieved and rinsed again thoroughly in cold water on the following morning before being tipped into a clean hook-on pot which can be attached to the mesh in the aviary shelter.

3 The container must be removed from the aviary in the afternoon and can then be washed out and dried, ready for use again the following day.

You can soak ordinary budgerigar seed although, alternatively, millet sprays can be used for this purpose. These consist simply of millet still in a seedhead and can be fed either wet or dry.

Water, too, needs to be supplied in containers that prevent the contents from being soiled. Tubular drinkers with special clips, which attach to the mesh, can be used for this purpose. Drinking bottles with ball-tipped stainless steel spouts are another option. In aviary surroundings, drinkers should be placed under cover where they are less likely to be contaminated by algal growth, and any supplement in the water will be less susceptible to being activated rapidly by exposure to sunlight.

During cold weather, the water will not freeze so readily if it is under cover in an insulated birdroom. At this time of year, particularly with drinking bottles, it is important to check that their contents are liquid. There may often be a plug of ice hidden within the spout, which will stop the flow of water, depriving the budgerigars of water as a consequence.

Grit and minerals

Although it has become more controversial over recent years, grit is generally considered to have an important part to play in the budgerigar's digestive process. Grit is stored in the gizzard, which is the area in the digestive tract before the intestines, where the seed is broken down. The particles of grit help to grind up the seed kernels, thanks to the muscular contractions of the walls of this organ, and prevent the food coalescing and causing an impaction here. There are two distinct types of grit.

■ **Mineralized grit** is relatively insoluble, even in the acid medium of the gizzard

Right: *Most budgerigars will consume grit, although normally only in small amounts. It can be dispensed easily with a scoop of this type.*

CHAPTER
FOUR

■ **Oystershell grit** dissolves quite rapidly, adding to the budgerigar's intake of minerals and trace elements, such as iodine, which is particularly important for the health of these birds.

Grit can be supplied in small containers, but the contents should be topped up regularly. Alternatively, it can be sprinkled lightly over the floor of the budgerigars' quarters. In aviary surroundings, where the floor is usually lined with sheets of newspaper which may be taped in place, the addition of some grit on top will help to lessen the risk of the sheets being disturbed as the birds fly around their quarters.

Another vital constituent that budgerigars require is cuttlebone or, alternatively, a calcium block. Seed is very low in terms of this vital element, which is a key component not just of the skeletal system but also eggshells. Therefore calcium assumes even greater importance during the breeding season. Like grit, cuttlebones can

Iodine supplements

Budgerigars should also be provided with an iodine supplement, usually in the form of a so-called nibble, which can easily be fixed up adjacent to a perch in a cage or aviary surroundings. Iodine itself is a trace element which is taken up and used by the thyroid glands, located in the vicinity of the neck. These glands are vital in regulating the body's metabolism, by means of hormones circulated in the blood. A likely sign of an iodine deficiency can be seen in budgerigars suffering from the condition described as being 'stuck in the moult', when pin feathers remain evident on the bird's head for much longer than usual.

Although these iodine blocks are often pink, it is better to choose white ones if possible, especially for exhibition budgerigars because, sometimes, the pink coloration may temporarily transfer on to a bird's facial feathering, which is not recommended before a show.

Right: *Cuttlebone is traditionally given to budgerigars to supplement their calcium intake, and it can also serve to keep their bills in trim.*

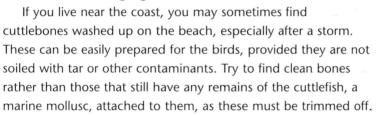

be purchased from most seed suppliers and need to be placed so that the soft, powdery side is easily accessible to the budgerigars.

If you live near the coast, you may sometimes find cuttlebones washed up on the beach, especially after a storm. These can be easily prepared for the birds, provided they are not soiled with tar or other contaminants. Try to find clean bones rather than those that still have any remains of the cuttlefish, a marine mollusc, attached to them, as these must be trimmed off.

Immerse the bones in a bucket of clean water at home, changing this twice daily over the course of a week or so. The cuttlebone should then be left to dry thoroughly in well-ventilated surroundings, after which it can be transferred to a cardboard box and stored until required. Budgerigars, especially hens, will consume much greater quantities during the breeding period, especially just prior to egg-laying.

Fresh foods and supplements

Staining of the feathering can also be a problem when offering carrot, which is a valuable precursor of Vitamin A, so exhibitors usually withhold this vegetable for a week before a show for this reason. Carrots should be peeled before being given to birds, and can either be grated or cut up into small pieces for them to nibble. Fresh green food is also valuable if offered regularly in small amounts. Avoid giving large quantities irregularly, however, since this is likely to cause diarrhoea as the birds gorge themselves on this delicacy. It must always be fresh and never wilting.

CHAPTER
FOUR

Powdered supplements

Powdered supplements generally contain a wider range of ingredients than those available in liquid form, which need to be added to the birds' drinking water. In either case, it will pay to check the expiry date, because you will use only a small amount, so buy from a store that has a high turnover to obtain the freshest stock at the outset. Always follow the instructions for use carefully, and do not overdose the birds, because this can be harmful if not fatal, especially over a period of time.

A variety of suitable wild and cultivated plants can be given to budgerigars, including the following:
■ Chickweed (*Stellaria media*)
■ Plants belonging to the dandelion family
■ Various seeding grasses.

Always check carefully when providing wild foods that they have not been sprayed with any potentially harmful chemicals. In temperate areas during the winter months, cultivated plants, such as spinach beet and cabbage, can be offered as well. Avoid green lettuce, however, as this contains little in the way of nutrients other than water – red lettuce is a better option.

Always wash greenstuff thoroughly and shake it dry before feeding it to your budgerigars. You can then tip a powdered supplement over it, as this will adhere well to the moist surfaces. Unlike many parrots, budgerigars generally show little interest in fruit, although they will eat sliced dessert apples, which offer a further opportunity to dispense a supplement of this type.

Always avoid offering wilted or yellowing greenfood, and be sure to remove any that is left uneaten at the end of the day, to prevent the risk of resulting digestive disturbances. If you can grow greenfood at home, even in a pot, you will then have a fresh supply available.

Taming and training a pet budgerigar

Young budgerigars between six and nine weeks old can usually
be tamed quite easily because they have no fear of people. It
is often possible to run your finger parallel with the perch and
simply persuade a young budgerigar of this age to step on to it.
If you carry on with this approach, your budgerigar should soon
sit readily on your hand in this way. You should also find that the
bird will start to take tidbits of food, such as part of a millet spray
held in your other hand, when it is perched here.

Above: *A budgerigar will always remain tame if it is obtained
as a pet at an early age.*

CHAPTER
FOUR

Safety in the home

The next stage in settling your pet into its new home will be to persuade it to behave in a similar fashion out of its quarters. First, you must ensure that the room is safe for it to be released. Young budgerigars, in particular, are likely to fly around wildly when they are first allowed out of their cage and can easily end up injuring themselves as a consequence. It is especially important to cover any windows with net curtains to indicate that there is a barrier here, as well as obviously ensuring that the windows themselves are closed. This prevents any risk of the budgerigar trying to fly through the glass barrier, or escaping.

Try to design the room overall with your bird's safety in mind. This will entail covering any fires as well as fish tanks. Remove potentially harmful plants, such as cacti with their sharp spines, or others that may be poisonous, like ivies. In fact, it may be safer to remove all house plants rather than risk your pet's health. Valuable ornaments should also be transferred elsewhere in the home, just in case they are knocked over and broken by the budgerigar. Always ensure that other pets, such as dogs and cats, are excluded, before letting your bird out.

You may want to fix some perches around the room, as this will make it easier for your budgerigar to find somewhere to land comfortably after flying around for a period. Special structures incorporating a perch which can be fitted on top of the budgerigar's quarters are available, as are various other free-standing toys of different designs. A budgerigar will soon be happy flying from perch to perch in the room, but persuading your pet to return to its own quarters can be difficult at first, without having to catch it.

It helps to establish a routine in this respect, allowing your budgerigar out to fly around at a set time each day when you will be home, preferably in the evening, and then encouraging it to return to its quarters just before you switch out the light. You may find that it will perch on your hand, assuming that it is now relatively tame, allowing you to transfer it back into its quarters in this way, but often what happens is that just as you reach the cage door, the bird flies off back into the room, often heading up to a higher vantage point, such as a curtain rail.

It is not a good idea to chase after your budgerigar, as this will be stressful for your pet. It is better to allow it to stay where it is and move a secure chair within easy reach of its vantage point. Then, having switched out the lights in the room and using a torch if necessary, climb up on to the chair and catch the budgerigar. With the room in darkness, it will be much easier to approach closely and it will then simply be a matter of carrying the bird back to its quarters.

You may decide to cover the cage for the night, as it has been suggested that effectively prolonging the day length by means of artificial lighting in the room can make budgerigars more susceptible to persistent moulting. It is important not to use a towel or similar item, however, because a budgerigar could easily become caught up by its claws in this material when it starts to climb around its cage. Special plastic covers designed to fit cages are a much safer option.

Right: *Budgerigars do show definite individual preferences in terms of toys. If necessary, try moving a toy that your pet shows little interest in, as it could be its position that is off-putting to the bird.*

CHAPTER
FOUR

Teaching a budgerigar to talk

Budgerigars rank as among the most effective mimics out of all the members of the parrot family, but the way in which they are taught to talk will influence their talking ability. Young birds, for example, are much easier to teach than adult birds, because at this age they are more responsive to sounds. They also appear to find it easier to mimic the sound of a female or a child's voice rather than that of a man, possibly because the pitch is nearer to their own.

When it comes to teaching budgerigars to talk, one of the most important attributes is patience. Here are some important guidelines to help you:

■ Only try to teach your budgerigar to talk in a quiet environment where there are no distractions or background noise of any kind.

■ Always repeat the chosen phrase slowly and clearly.

■ Keep the training sessions short – a maximum of about five minutes should be adequate – and repeat these sessions several times each day.

■ Stick to the same word or phrase. Chopping and changing will only confuse your bird.

■ Do not worry if your budgerigar fails to respond immediately. It is likely to take several weeks to see results.

■ You can record your voice on to an audio tape or CD, and replay it back to the budgerigar when you are out, but this will be less successful than talking directly to your pet.

■ Always teach a budgerigar to repeat your phone number and/or your address as a priority. If it escapes in the future, you will then have a much greater likelihood of being reunited with your pet, as anyone finding it should be able to contact you without difficulty.

Cleanliness

Most owners with pet budgerigars use sandsheets for their pets. These are produced in specific sizes to correspond to those of cages. Loose bird sand is an alternative, but this is relatively heavy and does not generally provide such an adequate covering. Clean sheets of newspaper are another option, weighed down by bird sand, but this does not appear as attractive as sandsheets.

Within the aviary, however, newspaper tends to be used more commonly on the floor of the flight, giving good coverage and being cheap, absorbent and relatively easy to dispose of in contrast to large amounts of bird sand. When they come into breeding condition, hen budgerigars will often start to rip newspaper or sandsheets apart, which can create more mess for a time, but this phase soon passes.

Above: *Spraying prior to cleaning the floor of the cage prevents feather dust being wafted into the atmosphere.*

Since budgerigars will often spend time on the floor of their quarters, even sometimes nibbling their droppings, it is important that this area is cleaned regularly. The flight area of the aviary will be partly washed down by rain, but it should still be scrubbed or hosed down regularly, using a special disinfectant to help prevent the spread of disease.

Holiday time

It is usually not too difficult to find someone to look after a pet budgerigar while you are away but, ideally, they should be used to birds and not have other pets, such as cats or dogs, that could harm your bird. It is also not a good idea to recommend that your bird is allowed out to fly around in strange surroundings while you are away. But transferring your pet temporarily to a new home will be a better arrangement than leaving a budgerigar on its own, because it will have human company. Should your friend already have a budgerigar, there is little worry that either bird will stop talking as a result of being kept within earshot of each other. Once back in familiar surroundings, your pet will carry on talking just as it used to, with your encouragement.

It is obviously not possible to move an aviary of budgerigars when you go away. If you belong to a local bird club, you may be able to team up with a fellow member who will look after your birds while you are away, and then you can simply return the favour in due course. Alternatively, you may be able to persuade a friend or neighbour to call in and attend to the birds' needs, giving them fresh water every day. Should you have a large seed hopper, this will probably not have to be topped up daily, but be sure to leave enough seed available, along with clear written instructions. Also, always write down your contact details so that you can be contacted in the event of an emergency, along with those of your vet.

Baths and bathing

There are a range of designs of
bath which are now marketed
for budgerigars. These often fit
around the door of a cage,
allowing the bird to hop in here
and then splash around in the
water. A closed design, made of
clear plastic can therefore be
recommended for this purpose,
to keep the surroundings dry.

Regular bathing once or
twice a week will help to keep the
budgerigar's plumage in good
condition, but not all of these
parakeets will use a bath supplied
for them. It may actually be
better to obtain a plant sprayer
for this purpose. Having removed

Above: *It may actually be necessary to bathe a budgerigar prior to a show if its plumage is dirty.*

the seed pots, you can spray your pet with a fine mist of water
droplets. Do not point the nozzle directly at the budgerigar, but
allow the water to fall like droplets of rain from above. It is a good
idea to carry out this task just before you clean the cage, as this
will also help to dampen down the
inevitable feather dust here which
may otherwise be wafted around
the room at this stage.

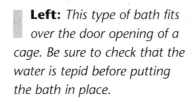

Left: *This type of bath fits over the door opening of a cage. Be sure to check that the water is tepid before putting the bath in place.*

CHAPTER FIVE

Breeding

*One of the great fascinations of breeding budgerigars is seeing
the chicks start to feather up and reveal their coloration in
due course. Budgerigars normally nest very readily, and most
pairs also make excellent parents, rearing the resulting chicks
without any difficulty. In fact, these parakeets can be so
prolific that pairs are normally not encouraged to rear more
than two rounds of chicks in succession without a break.*

B udgerigars have no fixed breeding season, reflecting their
habits in the wild where they nest opportunistically,
whenever conditions are favourable. Even so, especially in
an outdoor aviary, they should not be allowed to breed throughout
the year in temperate areas; this is because the chances of success
will be greatly reduced during the colder months of the year. If you
want to breed birds at this stage, they will need to be housed
indoors in a heated birdroom, with additional lighting supplied to
compensate for the shortened day length.

It is not hard to spot signs of breeding condition, with cock
budgerigars singing for longer periods, and tapping their bills
repeatedly on the perch. They will also feed hen birds and even
other cocks at this stage. In the case of hens, their ceres turn a
darker shade of brown, and they are likely to become more
destructive, attacking not just perches but also ripping apart any
lining paper on the floor of their quarters and destroying
cuttlebone more rapidly than usual.

CHAPTER
FIVE

▎Colony breeding

It is important to decide how you want to breed your budgerigars. The simplest and most straightforward option is to provide them with nest boxes in the aviary, rather than going to the trouble and expense of setting up breeding cages in the confines of a birdroom. Colony breeding is not without its drawbacks, however, and you will need to take steps to reduce the likelihood of fighting breaking out within the flock during the nesting period.

This is especially likely if you have a relatively large number of birds in a small aviary and do not supply them with sufficient nest boxes. Any upset to the dynamics of the colony will also increase the risks of aggressive behaviour, especially among the hens, which can easily have fatal consequences. At this time of

▎**Above:** *In these breeding cages, the boxes have been fitted outside the cage, giving the birds more space.*

year, it is not unknown for some individual budgerigars to even kill their companions in disputes over breeding sites.

Nest boxes

The positioning of the nest boxes themselves is important, as this can have a direct effect on the budgerigars' behaviour. They should all be fixed at the same height so as to avoid any fighting over the occupancy of higher boxes. The boxes should also be spaced out around the aviary, without the entrance holes abutting each other, because this can cause friction in some cases. Even if it does not progress to bloodshed, the squabbling that results will be stressful for the budgerigars and is therefore likely to have a detrimental effect on their overall breeding success.

Breeding results in aviary surroundings can also be affected by the weather, and it is important that the nest boxes are

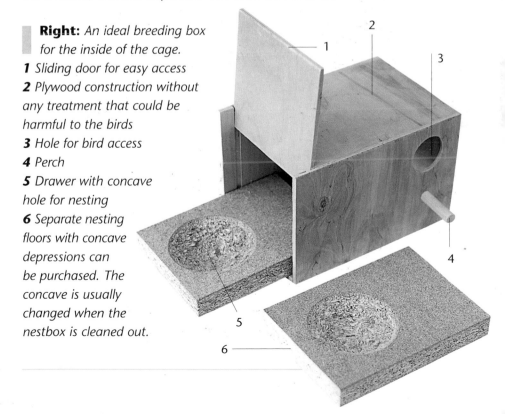

Right: *An ideal breeding box for the inside of the cage.*
1 Sliding door for easy access
2 Plywood construction without any treatment that could be harmful to the birds
3 Hole for bird access
4 Perch
5 Drawer with concave hole for nesting
6 Separate nesting floors with concave depressions can be purchased. The concave is usually changed when the nestbox is cleaned out.

CHAPTER
FIVE

Protecting the chicks

In the early days of budgerigar breeding, coconut husks were commonly used for nest sites, but now standard nest boxes are widely used. Made of plywood, these come equipped with a concave on the floor on which the hen will lay her eggs. Budgerigars do not require any type of nesting material, but it is important that the concave itself fits snugly in the nest box. Otherwise, there is a risk that newly-hatched chicks could slip down one of the sides, becoming fatally chilled as a result. The removable sheet of glass behind the outer sliding flap of plywood is also very important, because it will prevent chicks or eggs falling out when you want to look inside the nest box.

Above: *Budgerigar nestlings up to 14 days old. With eggs being laid on alternate days, there is often a gap of a week or more in the ages of the chicks in a nest.*

positioned under cover to prevent them from being flooded when it rains. It may be better to place them in the aviary shelter, because here they will not only be dry but are also less likely to be exposed to direct sunlight. Cats and other potential predators will not be able to disturb sitting birds so readily, and there are probably more vantage points to fix up the boxes. This can be carried out by means of brackets, screwed into place. It is important to fix the boxes where they are accessible, so that the interiors can be checked and cleaned easily.

❚ Pairings

It helps to prepare ahead for the breeding season, so that everything should proceed smoothly throughout this period. This is particularly important with colony breeding, as the best results will almost certainly be achieved if the flock is well established. This reduces the likelihood of disputes arising during the breeding season.

If you want to add to the colony, try to do so soon after the end of the previous breeding period rather than waiting until the budgerigars are about to nest again. Never put new birds in an aviary where others are already breeding as this may cause birds to desert their nests even if does not lead to direct conflict. It is not a good idea to leave unpaired birds, especially hens, in the aviary when pairs are nesting here – this is likely to result in these individuals proving disruptive. Removing them from the aviary beforehand will be safer.

Choosing a mate

Studies have revealed that budgerigars, unlike many parrots, do not form strong pair bonds. What often happens therefore is that once a hen has laid and is incubating her eggs, her mate will seek out other hens in the colony to mate with, although staying with his nesting partner. As a result, just because a pair of budgerigars

Above: *Colour-breeding cannot be guaranteed in an aviary, because budgerigars often prove to be fickle partners.*

are nesting together, there is no guarantee that their offspring will actually have been sired by that particular cock bird, especially as hens only need to mate once to fertilize their entire clutch.

If you are seeking to breed a particular pair within a colony, it is sensible to house them together in a cage for about a month, and then transfer them at the appropriate time into the aviary. They will hopefully stay together and breed in due course. The only other option, which is much more reliable, is to set up a breeding cage for them, with a nest box attached. In cases where the parentage of chicks is vital – when seeking to breed a particular colour or choosing pairings for exhibition purposes – this is the only way to ensure that the correct matings occur.

Breeding cages

It is possible to buy breeding cages or, alternatively, you can simply purchase the mesh front and construct a box-type cage around its dimensions. Remember to allow for a sliding tray for cleaning purposes to fit below the front, adding this figure to the overall height of the breeding cage. Although hardboard is sometimes used to make the sides of the cage, plywood is a much better option for this purpose. The interior of the cage should be painted with a light emulsion paint.

Plan the arrangement of the cages in the birdroom carefully, to avoid wasting space. Thus you may decide to fix the nest boxes on the front of the cages although they are more commonly fixed at each end, with a corresponding hole being cut through the side of the cage itself. You can buy nest boxes as well as breeding cages and other essential equipment from most good pet stores and bird farms.

Double breeding cages

These are often favoured over single units. These take the form of two separate fronts built into one cage, with a removable central partition between them, adding to their flexibility. This allows the double breeding cage to be converted easily to a stock cage after the breeding season; simply remove the central plywood partition and block off the nest boxes. But if you are constructing this type of cage yourself, you will need one nest box with an opening on the left-hand side, and another that has its access hole on the right.

Introducing birds to the breeding cage

Transfer the pairs into their breeding quarters ideally just before they start to show obvious signs of wanting to nest. Nevertheless, it may be worthwhile to shut off the nest box securely for about a week afterwards. Sometimes, especially if she is almost ready to lay, a hen will retreat into the nest box without allowing the cock bird to mate with her, and therefore the resulting eggs will prove to be infertile.

Breeding box perches

There should always be a short dowel perch beneath the entry point to a nest box. You will have to drill a hole at the corresponding position through the cage so that it can be fitted into the side of the box.

The perches assume great significance in the confines of the breeding cage, because if these are not fixed firmly in position, the budgerigars may not be able to mate successfully. Dowelling can be used for this purpose, being held in place at the back of the cage by means of small screws, and notched at the other end to fit snugly between the bars on the cage front. However, natural branches can be incorporated, thereby providing a more flexible alternative to fixed perches.

Egg-laying

It is usually possible to tell when egg-laying is imminent because the vent area of the hen becomes slightly swollen and her droppings become greatly enlarged for a short period of time. By this stage, she is likely to be spending long periods in the

Failure to hatch

Not all the eggs laid will hatch, often because they may be infertile. This can be checked by holding the egg up to a good light – a process sometimes called 'candling', as a candle was once used for this purpose. If you can see through the egg with the light behind it, then almost certainly, it was infertile. As a result of their appearance, such eggs are described as 'clear'. In cases where chicks developed but failed to hatch, possibly because they were too weak to cut their way out through the shell, then these are described as 'dead-in-the-shell'. This may reflect nutritional deficiencies in the budgerigars' diet.

nest box. Even after laying her first egg, however, she will not necessarily spend all her time here. This is quite normal behaviour, and although the incubation period for the first one or two eggs will be extended slightly, they will hatch closer together in due course. As a result, there will be less variance in size between the chicks, increasing the likelihood of survival of all the chicks. Cock budgerigars play no direct role in the incubation process, although they may spend time in the nest box alongside the hen.

Most hen budgerigars lay clutches of four to six eggs over the course of alternate days, although young birds laying for the first time and older hens may have smaller clutches. They are generally very reliable when incubating their eggs, and you can usually check the nest cautiously for short periods without any fear of the hen deserting her nest. It will help to distract her if you offer some greenstuff or a soaked millet spray perhaps, before seeking to look in the box.

Always develop a routine of tapping on the end of the box

Above: *A four-day-old chick. At this stage, its eyes are closed and it will have difficulty in maintaining its balance.*

CHAPTER
FIVE

Rearing foods

It is a good idea to provide budgerigars with softfood through the breeding period, especially when they have chicks. This type of relatively high protein food can be obtained in packeted form from seed suppliers, then tipped in small amounts into containers which hook on over the cage front near a perch. It will help to meet the nutritional requirements of the growing chicks. Soaked seed is another valuable addition to the diet of breeding pairs at this stage. You may also want to provide an additional water container as the adult budgerigars will be drinking much more than normal during this period.

before lifting the cover, as this will give the hen time to move off the nest. Otherwise, especially if the cock bird is in the box, it can end up as a mad scramble as both try to leave through the

access hole, resulting in eggs being scattered and damaged as well as chicks being displaced.

An absence of eggs

Most hens should lay within two or three weeks of being introduced to a breeding cage. If this does not occur, it is worthwhile transferring the pair back to the flight and allowing them to remain here for several weeks before trying again. A change of partner may also be advantageous in some cases, although compatibility is not usually a serious issue when breeding budgerigars.

Left: *This lining tray prevents any risk of young birds falling out when the nestbox is opened. The dummy eggs shown here are useful to curb egg-eating behaviour.*

Above: *Signs of feathering are now becoming apparent in these eight- and fourteen-day-old chicks. Their eyes have opened.*

Within the home, if you are trying to breed a single pair, the chances of success are likely to be lower, simply because budgerigars are social nesters by nature, and a pair of birds kept on their own may fail to breed. Recording and playing back the calls from an aviary of budgerigars can help to overcome this difficulty, and once the hen has laid, things normally proceed without any further worry.

In some cases, it may appear that the hen has not laid, whereas in reality, either she, her mate or both of them have eaten the eggs. Traces of shell and probably yolk on the concave are a tell-tale sign. This vice can usually be overcome by placing a couple of indestructible dummy eggs, as sold for canaries, in the nest. As a result, the budgerigars soon lose interest in behaving in this way, and the next round of eggs should be incubated without problems.

▍Nest box hygiene

CHAPTER
FIVE

As the chicks grow older, so their nest box becomes increasingly dirty, and it is a good idea to have spare concaves available so these can be changed at intervals when they are soiled. Dirty concaves can be left to soak for a few hours in a bucket of water and disinfectant, before being scrubbed off, rinsed and left to dry thoroughly, after which they can be used again in due course.

Changing the concave also provides an opportunity to check on the chicks. Pay particular attention to the state of their bills once they are about three weeks old. It is not unknown for food deposits to stick here, particularly in the notch of the upper beak or adjoining the tongue, and harden in position. The tissue of the bill is still quite soft at this stage and growing, which means that it can become easily distorted by such accumulations of food or even droppings.

This will lead to permanent malformation if it is not detected early, with the upper bill curling down inside the lower bill and being described as undershot as a result. Affected birds must have their bills trimmed back regularly for the rest of their lives, so it is very important to prevent this problem if possible.

Should you spot any deposits in the budgerigar's mouth, then you will need to remove the debris carefully, using the plain end of a matchstick.

▍**Left:** *Cleaning the inside of a chick's bill. Nest dirt here will cause permanent malformation.*

Ringing

You will need to decide at a relatively early stage whether you are going to band the chicks. This is important if you are intending to exhibit the birds, with breeders obtaining their own personalized rings from the budgerigar organisation to which they belong, so they can enter breeders' classes at shows. Closed rings can only be fitted while the young birds are in the nest, providing a reliable indication of when they hatched. In contrast, so-called split rings can effectively be clipped round the leg and are useful for identification purposes if, for example, you have two light green budgerigars in the aviary and need a way to distinguish between them.

1 Fitting a closed ring to a young chick is not especially difficult, especially once you have practised the technique. It is important to carry out the procedure with the chick resting securely on a table in good light, so you can see what you are doing. It is then a matter of bunching the three longest toes together and sliding the ring over them, up to the ball of the foot. The short fourth toe should be kept parallel with the back of the leg, and the ring should then be passed over this as well as the leg.

2 The final stage is to free the toe, using a blunt matchstick or similar tool, before checking that the ring will slide easily up and down this part of the leg above the foot. Ringing can usually be carried out once a chick is eight days old – if left too late, the foot will be too large to allow the ring to slide over it.

CHAPTER
FIVE

BREEDING PROBLEMS

In most cases, the breeding cycle proceeds without any problems, but occasionally difficulties may arise. Chicks sometimes die unexpectedly although feather problems are more of a general concern, especially French Moult.

Feather plucking

Most pairs of budgerigars prove to be exemplary parents but, occasionally, some turn out to be feather-pluckers. The reason for this behaviour is unclear, but it appears in part to be an inherited problem, affecting certain bloodlines more than others. All goes smoothly until the chicks are approaching three weeks of age and sprouting their feathers. Then, without any warning and within an hour or so, one or both of the adult birds will pick the emerging feather quills out from the skin of the chicks, denuding them especially over the back, although the affected area may be more

Above: *This chick has been attacked by one or both of its parents. This can happen when the adults are keen to nest again.*

widespread in some cases. This results in surprisingly little bleeding but, inevitably, severe bruising is likely to develop within a few days.

After behaving in this fashion, the adult birds will continue to rear their chicks normally. If you have a pair of budgerigars, at least one of which you know is a feather-plucker, you can use one of the sprays available to deter such behaviour. They need to be applied regularly to the chicks, starting just before they reach the vulnerable stage. Although budgerigars, like most birds, have a very restricted sense of taste compared with our own, the bitter nature of these products should deter them from attacking their chicks in this way. While plucked chicks leave the nest box missing feathers over their backs, these will grow again within a few weeks, and they will then be indistinguishable from other budgerigars.

French Moult

A feather problem that strikes at a slightly later stage is French Moult, so-called because it was first described in the huge French commercial budgerigar breeding establishments in the late nineteenth century. This is a potentially serious and now, unfortunately, widespread infection, whose cause remained a mystery for virtually a century. It is now known to be the result of a viral infection, although there is still no treatment available for the condition. It strikes chicks typically around five weeks of age, just as they are leaving the nest. They will shed their long flight feathers, as well as their tail feathers in some cases, and

Right: *A case of French Moult, as reflected by the loss of flight feathers along the back edge of the wing.*

are then unable to fly. Over the course of time, in mild cases, these feathers will regrow, but they tend to remain relatively fragile throughout the bird's life.

The infection can be spread easily when cleaning out nest boxes by using a brush that transfers the viral particles. Careful attention to disinfecting cleaning tools, as well as the concaves, is therefore vital in curbing its spread, while the use of an ionizer (see page 69) has been proven to lessen the ease with which this infection can transmitted in a confined air space.

It is not uncommon for odd cases of French Moult to crop up, with the flock of budgerigars presumably having some acquired resistance to the infection. However, sometimes, in a few instances, it can flare up and become a major problem, affecting almost all the chicks bred in a particular season. It is not a good idea to keep budgerigars that have been afflicted by French Moult for breeding purposes, but they can develop into excellent pets – the fact that they may not be able to fly strongly can actually be a bonus in certain domestic situations.

Weaning

Budgerigar chicks will normally have left the nest of their own accord by five weeks of age, although they will not be able to feed themselves at this stage, relying on the cock bird to take care of them for a few days until they are capable of eating independently. Almost certainly, the hen will have laid again by now, and it is important to wean the budgerigars before long, because otherwise they will persist in returning to the nest box. Here they will soil the new eggs, reducing the likelihood that these will hatch in due course. The young budgerigars should therefore be transferred to a large cage or flight where they have adequate space. You can then decide which birds you want to keep and which will not be required as part of your future breeding programme.

Right: *A feather duster. Such chicks have a significantly reduced life expectancy.*

Feather dusters

This much rarer condition, believed to have metabolic origins, is sometimes recorded, particularly in exhibition studs, and may be linked with a growth hormone disorder. It is recognisable when a chick in the nest seems to outpace its nestmates in terms of its rate of growth, but then, as its plumage emerges, it becomes excessively long over the body. As a result, such birds are now often known as feather dusters. There is no treatment possible for this condition, other than trimming back the plumage on the head to allow them to find food more easily. Feather dusters are also generally short-lived, with few surviving more than a few months.

Loss of an adult bird

Should one of the parents die during the breeding period, it may be possible to foster the eggs out to another pair that laid at a similar time. Mark them lightly with a pencil cross, so you can determine whether or not they actually hatch in due course. It is more serious, especially with young unfeathered chicks, if the hen dies, because she will be feeding them at this stage. Again, fostering may be possible but, failing this, the chicks will need hand-rearing, using one of the parrot hand-raising foods now available, and to be kept warm.

CHAPTER
FIVE

COLOUR BREEDING

One of the many fascinations of breeding budgerigars is the range of colours that may crop up. There are genetic rules that enable the likely appearance of chicks to be predicted. These are based on the fact that certain colours are dominant over others. This is why, over several years, an aviary of budgerigars breeding on a colony system will inevitably end up containing a higher percentage of green birds, since this colour tends to be dominant over other varieties.

Recessive characters

The genetic material responsible for an individual budgerigar's coloration is present within the nucleus of every living cell, in the form of genes located on structures called chromosomes. These chromosomes usually occur in pairs, with genes coding for a

Stud records

Record-keeping is very important in the development of a stud of budgerigars, and each breeding cage should have its own card detailing the following:

■ The pair housed
■ When and how many eggs the hen laid
■ The number of chicks hatched and reared successfully
■ Their colours and ring numbers for future identification.

This information can then be transferred to the stock register, which should allow you to trace the origins of all the budgerigars in the aviary. It will be vital in deciding how to pair your birds in the future. Breeders increasingly are using computers to store this type of information, and there are special software programmes, advertised in bird-keeping journals, to simplify this task.

Right: *The Recessive Pied is an example of a straightforward recessive mutation.*

characteristic, such as coloration, being present on both. These genes may match, or they may differ. When they are not the same, one is described as dominant because it will exert its effect over the other.

A pure Light Green budgerigar, for example, when paired with a Sky Blue budgerigar will have all green offspring. But, although not visually obvious, all these chicks will carry a Sky Blue on one of their chromosomes. This is because they receive one set of chromosomes from each parent. Then, in turn, if they mate with similar individuals, a percentage of their offspring will be Sky Blue. The full range of possible pairings under these circumstances is shown in the table below. When a budgerigar carries a recessive characteristic, such as Sky Blue, this is indicated by an oblique line. Such birds are often described by breeders as being split for Sky Blue, or carrying the Sky Blue factor.

Autosomal recessive pairings

Light Green — Light Green

100% Light Green

Light Green — Sky Blue

100% Light Green/Sky Blue

Light Green/Sky Blue — Light Green/Sky Blue

50% Light Green/Sky Blue + 25% Sky Blue + 25% Light Green

Light Green/Sky Blue — Sky Blue

50% Light Green/Sky Blue 50% Sky Blue

Light Green — Light Green/Sky Blue

50% Light Green/Sky Blue + 50% Green

Sky Blue — Sky Blue

100% Sky Blue

CHAPTER
FIVE

▌ Sex-linkage

One pair of chromosomes differs from the others in the cell nucleus. These are the sex chromosomes, which are responsible for determining an individual's gender. In cock birds, they are of corresponding length, but one of the pair in hens is distinctly shorter. As a result, some of the genes on the longer chromosome are unpaired. This means that such budgerigars cannot be split for sex-linked colours; their appearance in this instance corresponds to that of their genetic make-up. This has quite a marked effect as shown in the table below.

If you want to have the opportunity of breeding sex-linked offspring, therefore, you should use a sex-linked cock rather than a hen. Nor is it just colours that are sex-linked – opaline and cinnamon patterning both fall into this category.

Sex-linked recessive pairings

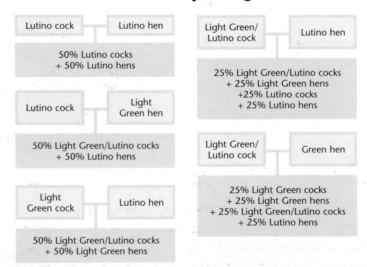

Lutino cock —— Lutino hen

50% Lutino cocks
+ 50% Lutino hens

Lutino cock —— Light Green hen

50% Light Green/Lutino cocks
+ 50% Lutino hens

Light Green cock —— Lutino hen

50% Light Green/Lutino cocks
+ 50% Light Green hens

Light Green/Lutino cock —— Lutino hen

25% Light Green/Lutino cocks
+ 25% Light Green hens
+25% Lutino cocks
+ 25% Lutino hens

Light Green/Lutino cock —— Green hen

25% Light Green cocks
+ 25% Light Green hens
+ 25% Light Green/Lutino cocks
+ 25% Lutino hens

Dominant mutations

Only a relatively few mutations are dominant, which means that a percentage of the resulting chicks in the first generation, known as F1, should be of this colour, although since chromosomes come together randomly, this cannot be guaranteed absolutely. When paired with a normal, if further normal individuals crop up in the nest, you can be sure that the parent budgerigar is a single factor (sf) rather than a double factor (df) individual. In the case of dark factor mutations (see page 19), however, it is possible to distinguish visually between single and double factor birds.

Dominant pairings

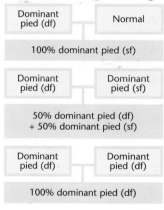

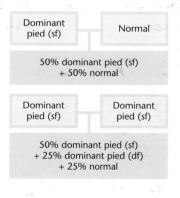

Crested mutations

It is usual to mate crested birds to non-crested ones, because of concerns that double factor crests cannot develop for genetic reasons. On average, half the chicks from pairings where one bird is crested should themselves be crested, but there can again be variances between individual nests.

CHAPTER SIX

Budgerigar health

Budgerigars, especially those kept as pets on their own, are usually quite healthy birds and may not require any veterinary attention throughout their lives. Most will live for at least six years and, in rare cases, budgerigars have been known to survive into their teens and even their twenties. When a bird does become ill, however, rapid veterinary attention will be required.

When a budgerigar appears ill, immediate action needs to be taken because its condition is likely to deteriorate rapidly. Consequently, you should always be watchful for the following signs of poor health:

- The bird appears less lively than usual
- Its plumage is no longer sleek but appears fluffed up
- It is eating less than normal, often simply sitting by its food pot
- Its droppings change in shape, colour or consistency
- It has laboured breathing, as shown by exaggerated tail movements, which may be accompanied by wheezing.

Prevention is always better than cure, and if you feed your bird a healthy diet and house it properly in clean surroundings, there is less likelihood of it developing any health problems. This risk is greater when a number of birds are housed together in aviary surroundings, which is why isolating new individuals at first is so important.

CHAPTER
SIX

▌ Treatment and recovery

Unfortunately, diagnosing avian illnesses accurately from such symptoms is very difficult, even for an experienced avian veterinarian without laboratory tests being carried out. Often, therefore, it is necessary to embark on a course of antibiotic treatment at the outset, in the hope of preventing the budgerigar's condition deteriorating to the point where it is beyond help. An injection of antibiotic given by a vet will speed up the budgerigar's recovery, and this is usually followed by further antibiotic treatment administered via the drinking water and sometimes the food as well.

The other essential that can make a vital difference to a sick budgerigar's recovery is warmth. If you have a large collection of budgerigars, you may want to invest in a special hospital cage with a thermostatic control for this purpose. This will allow the temperature not only to be raised but also lowered, allowing the sick bird to be reacclimatized gradually as its condition improves.

The type of food that you offer can also be significant in assisting the recovery of a sick budgerigar. Soaked millet sprays are often eaten by those birds recuperating from illness that refuse their regular seed mixture. Position the food near the bird, assuming that it is perching, because often a sick budgerigar will not venture to the ground in search of something to eat. It is also important to withhold all fresh food at this stage and to encourage the budgerigar to drink its medicated water, rather than relying on the fluid present in greenstuff and similar foods.

▌ **Right:** *Dark areas on the upper bill can result from minor internal bleeding here. This can often happen if a bird is frightened and flies heavily into the aviary mesh or a sheet of glass. The damage usually heals by itself.*

CHAPTER
SIX

COMMON AILMENTS

Budgerigars housed in groups in aviaries are far more vulnerable to illnesses than those kept on their own as pets in the home, simply because they are more likely to come into contact with potentially harmful bacteria and other microbes which can cause disease. It is not just cleanliness which is important in preventing illness, but also to quarantine new birds before introducing to them to the flight, to ensure as far as possible that they are healthy. Also, when a budgerigar does appear off-colour, it should be removed from the aviary at the earliest opportunities, not just to increase its chances of recovery, but also to safeguard the health of its companions as far as possible.

Above: *This budgerigar is not looking particularly well, as shown by the coloration of its cere. Abnormal changes of this type in birds are frequently linked with tumours of the reproductive organs or kidneys.*

Enteritis

This term is often used by breeders to describe birds that are suffering from digestive upsets, although it does not have a single cause.

■ **Symptoms** In most cases these are similar, with greenish droppings being a feature. The cause is often a bacterial infection, and affected birds should be kept in isolation to reduce the risk of the illness spreading. Sometimes just one bird may be affected, but if larger numbers are affected, there is a possibility that they could have acquired the infection from rodents, such as mice entering the aviary in search of food, and you will need to check accordingly. Live traps can be used to remove rodents safely from the aviary surroundings, followed by thorough disinfection.

Treatment: With a severe outbreak of enteritis, your vet is likely to advise that tests be carried out to try to isolate the organism, and autopsies can be helpful in this respect as well. By identifying the cause of infection, effective treatment can be given. It may even be worthwhile to have tests carried out on birds that have apparently recovered. The purpose of this is to check that they are not still infective and passing the organism responsible for the illness out in their droppings.

'Going light'

This term is used to describe birds that have lost weight and are appearing ill, with their breastbone feeling more prominent than usual. This can be the result of a long-standing illness, which it may not always be possible to treat successfully.

Tumours can be a common reason but there can be other causes of going light, including trichomoniasis (see page 122).

■ **Symptoms** One of the earliest signs of an internal tumour of this type will be a loss of weight, frequently linked with a change in cere coloration. The cere of an affected cock bird is likely to turn slightly brownish, particularly around the nostrils, whereas that of a hen becomes much paler than usual.

Treatment: In the latter stage, the budgerigar will lose its ability to perch and will then have to be put to sleep painlessly because there is no treatment for these tumours.

Eye inflammation

Either one or both eyes may be affected and it can be difficult to elucidate the cause without tests. Generally, if only one eye is inflamed, it is probably a minor problem, resulting perhaps from a scratch. If both eyes are affected and the bird shows other symptoms of illness, this may be indicative of a more serious generalized infection, such as chlamydiosis (psittacosis).

Eye ointments

Ointment tends to stain the plumage around the eyes but is generally easier to apply than drops. If these splash on to the eyelid as the bird blinks, they will not reach their target. When applying ointment, hold the bird for a few moments so the medication can start dissolving into the eye, rather than being wiped off immediately on to a perch. Due to the outpouring of tear fluid, ophthalmic treatments must be given several times daily to maintain a therapeutic level to overcome an infection.

■ **Symptoms** Although rare, this can be spread to people, causing symptoms resembling severe influenza. Should you have cause to suspect this infection, then contact an experienced avian vet for advice.

Treatment: Minor eye ailments can be treated using either ophthalmic drops or ointment, and the response to treatment is often very dramatic. Although the swelling and inflammation may subside within hours, continue the treatment so that there is no risk of the infection flaring up again.

Fatty lumps

These growths, called lipomas, are often encountered in middle-aged budgerigars, particularly those kept as pets.

■ **Symptoms** They are typically seen on or close to the breastbone, and can become sufficiently large as to protrude through the plumage itself. Worse still, even when smaller in size, they will affect the budgerigar's ability to fly any distance, causing the bird to flutter to the floor.

Treatment: It is important to be alert to the development of such lumps because, especially if detected early, they can now be removed quite successfully by surgery, allowing the budgerigar to continue flying normally. Certain bloodlines do seem more susceptible to these growths than others, however, and sometimes a lipoma will regrow again after being removed.

CHAPTER
SIX

▌Parasites

Budgerigars being kept in aviary surroundings are especially at risk from parasites, including the following:

Red Mite (*Dermanyssus gallinae*)

This can be spread easily by wild birds, especially young fledglings drawn to the aviary in the hope of finding food. Barely visible to the naked eye, these mites live mainly in the aviary or cages rather than on the budgerigars, which makes them harder to eliminate.

■ **Symptoms** Red Mites are a particular hazard during the breeding season if they gain access to nest boxes, because they can multiply rapidly here, emerging from their hiding places to suck the blood of both chicks and adult birds, which gives them their red coloration. Worse still is the fact that they can survive for months without feeding, allowing them to live from one breeding season to the next and to multiply rapidly in the following year when the nest box is in use again. Red Mites are likely to cause serious anaemia in the case of chicks and may also trigger feather plucking, because of the accompanying irritation caused by their bites.

Treatment: Good hygiene is therefore very important to prevent these parasites from becoming established. There are special, safe aerosols that can be used to spray both budgerigars and their surroundings to kill Red Mites, as well as special washes for breeding equipment and using around the aviary. Such treatments should be used regularly, in accordance with their instructions, to eliminate any risk of a build-up of these parasites. It is also a good idea to treat all new birds as a further precautionary measure.

Feather lice

Since these parasites spend all their time on the bird's body, they are reasonably easy to eliminate.

■ **Symptoms** If the plumage takes on a chewed appearance at its edges, and the budgerigars appear to be preening more than usual, then lice are the likely reason.

Treatment: Lice are killed by the type of spray described above, but these parasites are far less of a problem in budgerigars. This treatment has to be repeated to ensure that all stages in the life cycle have been killed.

Moulting

Although not actually an illness, moulting is a debilitating time for budgerigars, and often the stage when sickness is most likely to strike. The use of a tonic should help to speed a bird through this period, as the new feathers emerge wrapped up in feather sheaths. By preening and rubbing, so the budgerigar breaks down these waxy casings, allowing its new plumage to unfurl. If a bird moults constantly however, this can be a reflection of prolonged light exposure in the home, or a hormonal problem linked with the thyroid glands.

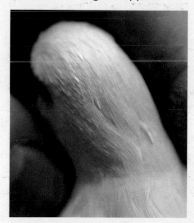

CHAPTER
SIX

Scaly face

A different type of medication is needed to overcome scaly face, another mite infection.

■ **Symptoms** Scaly face is most likely to be seen on and around the bill, although it can spread further on to the body in a few cases and may also affect the legs. These crusty growths need to be treated urgently to prevent any permanent malformation of the bill. Remove any affected individuals from the aviary for treatment. This is important as the mites may be spread by direct contact when the budgerigars are feeding each other, and possibly also from being deposited on perches as the birds wipe their bills here.

Treatment: The simplest method of treatment is to use a proprietary remedy available from pet stores, or petroleum jelly which will need to be wiped over the affected areas. This effectively suffocates the mites but must be repeated virtually on a daily basis until all signs of the mites have disappeared, which may take several weeks. The alternative is to use the drug known as ivermectin, which is available on veterinary prescription, diluted to the appropriate level for these parakeets. It is easily applied in drop form to the skin, usually on to the neck, with a single dose often proving adequate to kill the mites.

Trichomoniasis

Not all parasites are found externally on a bird's body. Budgerigars are especially vulnerable to a microscopic parasite known as *Trichomonas*, which localizes in the bird's crop. However, affected birds may not show symptoms.

■ **Symptoms** In adult birds, it can cause what appears to be vomiting, with an unpleasant yellowish mucus being regurgitated and often staining the plumage around the bill and even on the forehead. Affected individuals frequently spend longer than normal apparently eating, but on close examination of the food pot, you will see they have only been dehusking the seed rather than swallowing it. This will be particularly apparent with plain canary seed, since the outside of the kernel is much darker in appearance than the husk.

Treatment: When the crop (located at the base of the neck) is felt in the case of a budgerigar suffering from trichomoniasis, it will be swollen and full of gas. Hold the budgerigar upside down and gently massage the crop in the direction of the head to milk out the gas. This will aid the bird's recovery, although specific medication added to the drinking water to kill the parasites is also important.

Note: Young budgerigars are actually much more susceptible to the effects of trichomoniasis than adults. They will frequently die with few if any previous symptoms not long after becoming independent; the most evident sign in this instance is likely to be weight loss. The parasites are spread easily between birds by regurgitation of the contents of the crop, so if you have had a number of budgerigars affected, it can also be worthwhile treating all of them in the aviary. As a precautionary measure, you can add medication to the drinking water under veterinary advice. This should be carried out well before the start of the breeding season in the hope of eliminating these parasites permanently from the flock.

CHAPTER
SIX

FIRST AID

There are occasionally times when you will need to take action to protect your pet's life, but it is important to remember that budgerigars do suffer from stress when in shock, and excessive handling should be avoided at this stage. The best thing to do is to remove a bird from any danger, make it comfortable and leave it to recover quietly.

In some cases, this may be all that can be done, especially when a bird has flown hard into a window pane, for example, and stunned itself. Faced with this situation, the best thing that can be done is to transfer the budgerigar to the darkened environment of a box lined with tissue paper where it will hopefully recover, before transferring it back to its quarters. Sadly, however, it may suffer a fractured skull as a result of the collision and this is likely to be fatal.

Cat bites and blood loss

Medical intervention may be required in some cases of injury, particularly when a budgerigar has being rescued from a cat. Cats have very unpleasant bacteria in their mouths and, via their sharp teeth, they effectively inject these into the bird's body, leaving it at risk from a potentially fatal infection. Protective antibiotic cover will give the best insurance against your bird succumbing to these bacteria, but because it will be in a state of shock, handling needs to be kept to a minimum at first.

The same applies if you rescue a budgerigar that has been attacked by one of its companions, although the risk of a serious infection is significantly lower in this case. Leave the bird in a warm, quiet place to get over the worst of the shock. An avian electrolyte product added to the drinking water should aid recovery at this stage.

It is a myth that losing just a few drops of blood will be fatal to a budgerigar, but if a claw is bleeding, you can trigger the clotting process by pressing a finger over the cut end for a few moments. Similarly, some breeders will use a styptic pencil, as sold for minor shaving nicks, to apply to the damaged tip of the claw under these circumstances.

Ring removal

In most cases, a ring causes no problems once it is in place, but occasionally, especially in middle-aged budgerigars, the leg may start to swell up around it. This is a serious condition for which the only solution is the removal of the ring since, otherwise, the budgerigar will ultimately lose its foot. Taking off a closed ring is not an easy task, requiring special cutters, and the greater the degree of inflammation around and under the ring, the harder this task becomes. If you suspect that a bird's leg is becoming swollen, contact your vet so that the ring can be removed at the earliest opportunity. This may require an anaesthetic.

Egg-binding

Pet birds housed on their own can sometimes be affected by this condition, although it strikes more commonly in the case of breeding pairs. Egg-binding is always serious and can easily become life-threatening in affected hens. A hen suffering from egg-binding usually leaves the nest box and perches for a period, although looking unsteady on her feet. Before long, she will have lost the ability to perch and will be huddled up on the floor of the aviary, with her condition deteriorating rapidly. Gentle handling may allow you to feel the egg trapped in her body. This obstruction must be removed urgently, if possible without being broken because this increases the likelihood of subsequent

FIRST AID

CHAPTER
SIX

infection developing in the reproductive tract.

The best solution is to arrange for your vet to examine the hen as an emergency and to give her an injection of calcium borogluconate. This is usually sufficient to allow the smooth muscle to contract effectively and force the egg out of her body. Should this fail, surgical removal is likely to be necessary. The egg itself may be abnormally large or, often, soft-shelled with a rubbery coating. This suggests that the hen may be suffering from a calcium deficiency, so pay particular attention to her diet. Soluble calcium may even be recommended. It is not a good idea to allow a budgerigar that has suffered from egg-binding to breed again until the next breeding season, in order to give her the opportunity to recover fully from her illness.

Cutting the nails and bill

This can be necessary on occasions, particularly with pet birds, but if you are nervous or unsure about this task, ask your vet for advice, especially in the case of the bill.

■ **Nails** It is important to use a stout pair of clippers rather than relying on a pair of scissors which are more likely to split the nail rather than cutting cleanly through it. The task must be carried out in good light, so that you can see the blood supply to the claw. This is visible as a thin pinkish streak running down the centre of the nail. You need to cut a short distance after this streak disappears, just removing the very tip of the claw where this is starting to curl round.

■ **Bills** Cutting the bill is more difficult but can be carried out in a similar way. It is most commonly required in the case of birds with undershot bills, which causes the lower bill to grow out in front of the upper part. Unfortunately, it is likely that the bill will need cutting back regularly throughout the budgerigar's life under these circumstances – approximately every two months.

USEFUL ADDRESSES

Most countries have their own national budgerigar societies. Their web sites also provide an easy way to find regional clubs and associations in your area which are affiliated to the national organisation.

UK
The Budgerigar Society Spring Gardens, Nottingham NN1 1DR
http://www.budgerigarsociety.com

USA
American Budgerigar Society
Membership secretary Marion Blake, 1302 E 77th Street, Indianapolis IN 46240
http://www.aviarybirds.com

The Budgerigar Association of America
http://www.budgerigarassociation.com

CANADA
The Budgerigar and Foreign Bird Society of Canada Inc.
http://www.bfbsbirdclub.org

AUSTRALIA
Australian National Budgerigar Council
http://www.budgerigarrare.com

DENMARK
Dansk Undulat Klub
http://www.nethotel1.dk

FRANCE
AFO
http://www.afoperruchesondulees.free.fr

GERMANY
DSV
http://www.dsv-ev.de

NETHERLANDS
Budgerigar Society Holland
http://www.home01.wxs.nl

INTERNATIONAL
World Budgerigar Organisation
http://www.worldbudgerigar.org